HAVE YOURSELF A PESKY LITTLE CHRISTMAS

HAVE YOURSELF A PESKY LITTLE CHRISTMAS

A Decade of Christmas and New Year Poetry

WILLIAM FRASER

Pesky Publishing Ltd

Pesky Publishing Ltd

www.peskypoetry.com

ISBN 978-1-7396901-2-0
EISBN 978-1-7396901-3-7

Copyright © William Fraser 2023

All rights reserved. This book or any portion thereof may not be reproduced or used in any manner without the express written permission of the publisher except for use of brief quotations in a referencing format.

PeskyPoetry, PeskyPoet, Pesky Publishing and all variants thereof are the Copyright of William Fraser and subject to a Trademark.

Cover artwork by Jenny Sprenger. All artwork is subject to copyright.

1st *Edition*

First Printed: 2023
PeskyPoetry (info@peskypoetry.co.uk)

Contents

	1
Dedication	2
Acknowledgements	3
Christmas Countdown 2012	4
Christmas Countdown 2013	19
New Year Countdown 2013	46
Christmas Countdown 2014	55
Christmas Countdown 2015	81
New Year Countdown 2015	112
Christmas Countdown 2016	115
Christmas Countdown 2018	141
New Year Countdown 2018	170
Christmas Countdown 2019	174
Advent Countdown 2019	203
New Year Countdown 2019	208
Christmas Countdown 2020	218

Advent Countdown 2020	249
New Year Countdown 2020	254
Christmas Countdown 2021	264
Advent Countdown 2021	290
New Year Countdown 2021	295
Christmas Countdown 2022	305
Advent Countdown 2022	332
New Year Countdown 2022	337
What Next?	348
About The Author	351

Dedication

To those who always pushed me to be myself and continue writing. This book, with over ten years of Christmas Poetry, is testament to your support. And mostly, to those who said I couldn't write, thank you for the scathing support.

Acknowledgements

As with all my work I would like to acknowledge those who have guided and supported me along the way. Without you, there would be no Pesky Poet.

Christmas Countdown 2012

It all started in December 2012. A naïve young university student barely away from the call of home. Under the name Creatively Become Indifferent I set out to share some silly Christmas poems in an advent calendar way. Not sure of how the format should work it was a case of doing two weeks of poems up to the 25th. Little did I know that these poems would be so popular...

December 11th — A Post a Day

For this year,
I want to share,
A post a day,
Up until,
The magical Christmas day,
Where I will share,
My very special day,
The day of Christ,
With you my readers.

December 12th — My Thanks to You

Day two today,
And I want to say,
Thank you all,
For the past six months.
*

Thanks for,
Your reading,
Your interest,
Your likes and shares,
Have not gone unnoticed,
And here is to the coming year.

December 13^(th) — My Year

I came,
I saw,
I wrote on this blog,
And what has 2012 taught me.
*

I learned of love,
I made new friends,
I had some laughs,
I have also fallen,
But in the end,
I learned its ok just to be me.

December 14th — A Letter to Santa

A letter to Santa,
Is but a wish,
A dream for Christmas day.
*

A request of the heart,
A prayer some might say,
But for me this year,
It's one of thanks,
As it feels like Christmas,
Each and every day.

December 15th — Last Year Today

Think all the way,
Back to last year,
And what do you have to say.
*

For me there's thanks,
And cheers,
And joy,
And memories of amazing days.
*

If I had to choose,
Just one thing to share today,
It would have to be,
Finding the one I love each and every day.

December 16th — PewDiePie

This year I discovered,
Something I must share,
Someone amazing at what he does.
*

He makes you laugh,
At horror games,
And reminds you,
Not to fear the dark.
*

He has a way,
Of playing games,
That will make you watch for hours.
*

So today I'd like to give it up,
for the one, the only, PewDiePie.

---

*Editor Note: this was written in 2012. I had no idea what would happen in the years to come. This poem is here purely for completeness.

December 18th — The Birth of Blue

Two months ago,
I built a bear,
At the build a bear factory.
*

His name is blue,
He is a husky,
And he is my companion,
On the long cold winter nights.
*

He is so cute,
Sitting on my bed,
While I study away,
And write to you.
*

Have fun my readers,
And don't under estimate,
The power of a teddy bear.

December 19th — Lost For Ideas

I have found myself lost lately,
Lost for ideas,
In this vast world,
How is that possible.
*

There is the amazing white snow,
The beautiful red breasted sparrow,
The warm roaring log fire,
The gifts and the friends.
*

Isn't it great,
Now enjoy your day… Have fun.
Only 6 sleeps till Kris Kringle comes.

December 20th — The Presents the Gifts

It's that time of year,
Where we all look for cheer,
And find gifts for friends.
*

Not always easy to know,
What your friends are looking for,
But whatever it is,
You know that it will be "the best"
*

So, you take the gift home from the shop,
Wrap it with the greatest care,
And help that bow tied box,
Find its new carer.
*

The box will wait under the tree,
Until that exciting day,
Where your friend will open it and have,
A happy Christmas day.

December 21st — *It's Almost Christmas Day*

Jingle Bells,
My heart swells,
It's almost Christmas day,
Present made,
Kids all sleep,
As Santa packs his sleigh.

December 22nd — I think I've Lost My Way

Dashing through the snow,
I think I've lost my way,
I love the Christmas halls,
Especially Christmas day.
*

Bells in my head ring,
Making my head spin,
What fun it is to run and play,
X-box games tonight.

December 23rd — Have You Got

Have you got your Christmas turkey?
Fa la la la la, la la la la.
All the stuffing and the trimming,
Fa la la la la, la la la la.
*

It's all sitting in the freezer.
Fa la la, la la la, la la la.
Waiting for the Christmas morning.
Fa la la la la, la la la la.
*

Kids excited for the presents,
Fa la la la la, la la la la.
And everyone has gifts to share,
Fa la la la la, la la la la.
*

Let's all sing in joy together,
Fa la la la la, la la la la.
And forget about the weather,
Fa la la la la, la la la la.

December 24th — Christmas Eve

It's Christmas Eve,
Let the cheer Commence.
The countdown has started for the kids,
No less.
And in less than a day,
We will all say,
Merry Christmas to all,
And have a good day.

December 25th — Christmas Day for All

So, I have had chance to play,
Now I have chance to say,
Thank you all,
By reading this you have made my day.
*

All the presents are unwrapped,
The dinner turned into snacks,
And almost time to lay down my head,
But I will write to you before I head to my bed.
*

Even with all the presents,
And all the rosters,
Today wouldn't have been complete,
Without my family there,
To meet and greet.
*

I hope you all had a merry Christmas,
And we now lead into a kind new year,
To all the people in the world,
I raise a glass and sing a small cheer.

Christmas Countdown 2013

Following the success of 2012, still under the name Creatively Become Indifferent, and following an excellent year of writing poetry and short stories, I set myself the challenge to write another Christmas Countdown. This time covering the whole 25 days of December to Christmas. The result of 2013's countdown was a trebling in subscriptions and five fold increase in readers. With that, the idea of the Christmas Countdown had been set and became part of my poetry portfolio, or my poetfolio if you will.

December 1st — Christmas Countdown

Where has this year gone,
Come again is another December,
Gone now is the November.
***

Soon to come is the end of the year,
And with this there is the Christmas cheer,
So to the future, Christmas, and New Year.
***

Again this year,
I intend to spur on Christmas cheer,
By giving a countdown right up to New Year.

December 2nd — Puzzle Number One: Riddle Me This

What am I in the morning?
But not in the night,
I make the cocks crow,
And the first morning light,
I am only once a day,
365 days of this year,
I get earlier in the summer,
Later in the fall,
And I am well known,
For showing the new day is here.

December 3rd — Jack Frost

There's a nip in the air,
And some ice over there,
The windows are foggy,
And the roads are all slippy,
Jack Frost has been busy,
Making the cold,
Now in the night,
It might snow,
So wrap up warm,
When you go out,
And remember to sing,
"Let it snow, let it snow, let it snow!"

December 4th — Keep Me Warm

The cold is back this year,
And I have you hear,
Stay with me the night,
Keep me warm from the cold.
***

Please stay with me,
And never leave me,
Stay with me the winter,
Stay with me forever.
***

Please don't just be a Christmas dream,
Say you will never leave me,
Kiss me and take me tonight,
And cuddle with me through the night.
***

I will keep you warm,
And never let the cold get you,
If you will just be mine,
I will never leave to be lonely.

December 5th — Friends

Friends are what make life so fun,
Friends are the ones that fill in your time,
Without friends life would be dull,
So thank you friends for making life so amazing,
And let's hope that tomorrow will bring more fun.

December 6th — *Sing Sweet Melodies*

Sing sweet melodies of Christmas times,
Let's all remember last Christmas,
And the Christmases to come,
***
Sing sweet melodies of mulled wine,
And decorating halls,
For the holidays to come.
***
Sing sweat melodies of friends,
And of the times,
Spent together no matter the weather.
***
Sing sweat melodies of all the fun,
That this year brung,
Just because we can.

December 7th — Snow Day

Hip Hip Hooray,
It's a snow day.
Gone is the rain,
In is the snow games.
Snow balls are readied,
For the winter wars.
Out are the gritters,
Clearing the roads.
So peaceful and calm,
The countryside looks,
On this a beautiful snow day.

December 8th — Snow Globe

Shake that snow globe,
Give it a wish,
Let old Saint Nick,
Know what you want for Christmas,
***
Don't miss that mistletoe,
Come on give me a kiss,
You never know,
You could be my wish.
***
Don't say no to a night,
Sat by the fire,
With me in your arms,
And your wish of our kiss.

December 9th — Puzzle Number Two

Some people make me,
No one can hide from me,
Often I'm thrown,
With hands in gloves,
***
But with some coal,
And just a scarf,
Like magic I,
Look like a man.
So what am I?

December 10th — International Human Rights Day

Look to your left,
Now to your right,
Humans all around you,
Need a thought tonight,
Think of the pain,
Think of the dreams,
All humans around the world,
Are equal in each way,
Give a moment to them,
And make a difference,
Everyone has the right,
To a dream,
To a life,
And to be safe,
So give a thought,
Especially in this season of snow
Especially today,
On Human Rights Day.

December 11th — Christmas List

Snow and glitter and castor sugar,
All fall in copious quantities.
Boxes and bottles and buckets,
Full of gifts are carted around,
Hats and scarfs and gloves,
Have been out for over a month now,
Holly and mistletoe and glittery balls,
All deck the halls in this happy and joyous time.

December 12th — Holly Reef

Happy holidays,
One and all,
Let the joy ring out,
Leave the hate behind,
Yesterday is history let's look to tomorrow.
***

Remember this is the season,
Everyone should smile,
Extend a hand of friendship,
For you are only here for a while.

December 13th — Christmas Meets Halloween

Imagine a scene,
Christmas meets Halloween,
The thirteenth has fallen,
As the Christmas shoppers all swarm,
***

The horrors and sights,
Are not witches or frights,
But carollers singing their song,
***

So keep a watchful eye open,
And remember what is to come,
On this Christmassy Halloween.

December 14th — Monkey Day

Hay hay todays a good day,
Welcome to the day,
Where monkey business is ok,
December the 14th,
Is Monkey Day.
***

Get out of the house,
And play in the snow,
Or if there is none,
Just have some fun,
For today is the one day a year,
It ok to make light and merry,
And be a little monkey.

December 15th — Ten Days to Go

Ten days to go,
And by now you all know,
Christmas is coming close,
And so is the snow,
In comes the cold,
Out comes the coal,
As the cold takes its toll.
***
Thermoses are filled,
Drinks are no longer chilled,
And the garden no longer has a rose,
But we wait in delight,
For that one starry night,
With only ten days to go.

December 16th — Santa Claus

Santa Claus even if not here,
Brings joy to kids,
Every Year,
***
With his reindeer and sled,
And shiny bald head,
He comes out each year,
***
In supermarkets and stalls,
And even school halls,
His sits and waits this year,
***
He'll soon be on his way,
After stalking his sleigh,
And Christmas Eve is here.

December 17th — Christmas Plans

There are snowmen,
With snow balls,
Rudolf calls,
And we deck the halls.
***
We shake hands,
Make Christmas Plans,
Sing Psalms,
And meet our grans,
***
While I write poetry,
We sing happily,
Smile profusely,
Living our Christmas plans.

December 18th — Christmas to Me

There are the Christmas tunes,
There is a turkey in the oven,
There's a smile on the faces,
A laugh coming from the table,
There are the lights on the tree,
And let's not forget the company,
This is what Christmas means to me.
People all around the world feel as one,
All link arms together and thank everyone,
Remember the hardships of the past,
And the hardships to come,
But not focus of the hard times,
But look forward to the fun,
This is what I dream Christmas to be.

December 19th — Puzzle Number Three: Someone in Your Chimney

Someone in your chimney,
After the kids have gone to bed,
Night comes and he arrives,
Time to lay out the presents
And let the excitement begin,
***
Cause he arrives,
Late in the night,
And brings all the fun,
Ushers Christmas morning in,
So who am I?

December 20th — In the bleak UK

In the bleak mid economy, Frosty old people may moan.
People hard as iron, dead in their home.
Government had failed, their people, their people.
In the bleak mid economy, Cameron stays warm.

December 21st — Hanukkah

It's Hanukkah,
And I know what I wanna da'
It's a time for remembrance,
It's a time for enlightenment.
***
Even if you don't observe it,
We have all heard it,
And so I raise this to everyone,
Have a happy Hanukkah.

December 21ˢᵗ — *Solstice*

Another year has come to this,
A year today we thought,
We would all be in bits,
2012 came and went,
2013 draws to an end.
***

At the time of posting,
The earth is at its most winter,
And now the spring return begins,
The Winter Solstice is here,
Let us all join the celebrations.

December 22nd — Here's to Christmas

Here's to the tree,
Standing so proudly,
Decorated in all the fineries,
***

Here's to the gifts,
All stacked neatly,
Just waiting for Wednesday,
***

Here's to the parents,
Running off their feet,
Finding gifts for the kids,
***

And here's to the kids,
All excited and cheery,
Waiting for Santa's visit.

December 23rd — Christmas Week

So here we are,
It's now that week,
Christmas is near,
And the weather is bleak.
But although the weather is bleak,
And the snow may be cold,
Let's all remember the family we have,
And give a thought to those you know.
Forget family feuds,
And let the past go,
Remember family are family,
No matter what they do.

December 24th — Christmas Eve

Come all ye faithful,
Have a drink and laugh with us,
Right now is the night,
In come the cheers,
So tomorrow will bring the joy,
Tots with toys full of noise,
Mothers and fathers searching for batteries,
And not a soul should feel sad,
Singers of carols will fill the air.
***
Everyone everywhere,
Ventures out to the family houses,
Each to greet and wish a Merry Christmas.

December 25th — *Christmas Day Thank You*

Merry Christmas one and all,
Welcome to the new day,
Let's us toast to the turkey,
And give thanks for the gifts.
***
Let's give thanks to the people who cooked the meal,
And let us not forget the dishes.
We will all be tired come tonight,
So let's enjoy the day while it's light.
***
Christmas wouldn't be Christmas,
Without the friends and family,
And of course to me that includes you,
Thank you for reading, Merry Christmas to you,
***
Now get back to your Christmas,
And enjoy your day,
Join me tomorrow,
Until New Year's Day.

New Year Countdown 2013

After a very successful Christmas Countdown the creative juices were still flowing... Although the countdowns are generally written July to November now and signed off before the 1st of December, back in 2013 I was only up to two days ahead at any time. As a university student I loved this short deadline approach and the risk of missing a poem, but that is too much for me now as a full time worker. Did you notice the missing poem in the 2013 Christmas Countdown?

December 26th — Is Christmas Done?

Well that's it,
Christmas Day is done,
The hangover has begun,
***
The dishes put away for another year,
The chimney no longer the centre of the room,
The tree is no longer cluttered underneath,
And although Santa won't be there soon,
You now have presents to keep,
***
Now that Christmas Day is gone,
Don't let this be Christmas Done,
Let's take the joy of yesterday on,
And refill the rum for the New Year is yet to come.

December 27th — *Still Eating Turkey*

Every year,
Without any fear,
This day comes,
And we all jeer.
***

The turkey sits,
Still to be eaten,
On that plate,
In the fridge.
***

Mayonnaise and bread,
The meat's best friend,
Sit patiently waiting,
For every meal.

December 28th — Beyond the New Year

Beyond the shores of Aberdeen,
Is the boy of my dreams,
He lives in blissful ignorance,
And doesn't notice me.
***
Beyond the thoughts in my mind,
Is a feeling I can't describe,
No vocabulary on earth,
Could do justice to how I feel inside.
***
Beyond our friendship,
I don't see anything,
But I live in hope that one day,
He will say yes to me.
***
Beyond the New Year,
Maybe we I'll go out,
But only time will tell,
And it will be for the best no doubt.

December 29th — New Year Time

Time to sing our,
Auld Lang Syne's,
And remember the days gone by,
***

Time to remember,
The friends we've made,
And forget the ones we've lost,
***

Time to throw,
That turkey away,
And get rid of the Christmas food,
***

Time to write,
New Year's resolutions,
Even if keeping them is not always true
***

Time to shake,
The hands of our brothers and sisters,
And remember we are all human underneath,
***

So at the hour,
Raise your glass,
And a toast to the New Year.

December 30*th* — Puzzle Number Four: New Year Riddle

I'm what you do,
Come New Year,
The term you use,
For when someone near,
Is the first to walk?
Through your door,
With one gift,
And sometimes more.
It is said to be,
Bad luck to do,
This and bring nothing new.

December 31st — New Year

N is for the new things to come,
E is for everything we have done,
W is for wishes to be granted this year,
***
Y is for the yesterdays you will always remember,
E is for the end of this year,
A is for the after party at the bells,
R is for the rest of your life to come.

December 31st — Here It Comes

As this year draws to a close,
We remember stories of the old,
Laugh at jokes of the past,
And share mentions of hopes to come,
***
Mentions of Lions and Lambs,
And New Year's plans,
All with their New Year's resolutions.
***
So here she comes once again,
Showing we all move through time the same,
The clock comes close to that midnight chime,
Where we will all recognise the passage of time,
***
So tick tock goes the clock,
And time continues to move,
Tick tock goes the clock,
Now here's to the new.
***
So until next year,
I bid you adieu.

January 1st — Happy New Year

Happy New Year,
Let's all sing a cheer,
Gone is the old,
But let us not fear,
For tomorrow is new,
And although the time flew,
It will be better than last year,
***

My poems will still flow,
My blog will still breathe,
Now that I know,
You are all here to read,
Let this year bring,
All our desires and wants,
To the coming year,
Let us all sing at once.
***

!!!HAPPY NEW YEAR!!!

Christmas Countdown 2014

Thinking back on 2014 is a strange thing. My world changed completely and life got a lot busier. I left university to enter the world of work full time and even moved in with my future husband. But, even through that all, I kept up my writing projects and compiled yet another Christmas Countdown with some noticeable missing dates. The New Year Countdown did take a hit. Probably because it is not as popular as Christmas, the New Year Countdown was not as successful and was not continued in 2014.

December 1ˢᵗ — Another Year

Jingle Bells,
Another Year,
Let's all get jolly,
Let's give a cheer,
***
The first of December.
Is now here,
Let's all be jolly,
Let's all enjoy Christmas this year.

December 2nd — Presents

Wrapping paper all unrolled,
Christmas presents all lined up,
Time to start the tricky task,
Of getting paper all to match,
***
Pull up a seat,
And park up the tape,
Grab the scissors,
And get ready to wrap.

December 3rd — Riddle 1

I live in the north,
With good old St Nic,
I have four hooves,
Which I rarely use,
***

My name is often used,
To mean a woman,
Whose words are witty,
And her charm sharp,

Who am I?

I am Vixen

December 5th — *Special Dates of Christmas*

Here's some dates to make you jolly,
Some facts of Christmas past.
***

Did you know the 25th,
Was first celebrated in 440 AD.
***

The last white Christmas,
Was in 2008,
***

Christmas cake in the 19th Century,
Was munched on Christmas Eve.
***

And here is one for historians,
Oliver Cromwell banned Christmas in 1947
(This ban was lifted in 1960)

December 6th — Snowflake Lament

All cold and sharp,
White and bright,
The crystal of crystals,
All bright in the night.
***
A snowflake is light,
And is clear in the light,
Seamlessly in flight,
But delivers a bite.
***
Unsurpassed beauty,
Comparable to none,
With white crystals,
That are destroyed by the sun.

December 7th — Cold Winter Nights

Between the autumn and spring,
Between November and March,
The best place to be,
Is between the sheets,
All huddled up warm,
With your onesie on,
Don't let cold will bite,
On the winter nights.

December 8th — The Remastered Christmas Song

Baubles hanging from the Christmas tree,
Pine needles falling to your toes,
Presents underneath the tinsel tree,
We can see Christmas is all go,
***

Everybody knows friends and family,
Help keep the season bright,
Presents and sweets all lined up,
Waiting until after Christmas night

December 9th — *Snowflakes*

Snowflakes Glisten,
People listen,
To carollers outside their door.
***
Mince Pies beckon,
To be eaten,
As a Christmas time treat,
***
fifteen sleeps,
Till eyes peek,
At the Christmas presents in store.

December 10th — Riddle 2

I am like a dumpling,
All round and moist,
To have Christmas without me,
Is not a choice,
***

Christmas would not be complete,
Without a piece of me.
I come with alcohol,
Or alcohol free,

What am I?

I am Christmas Pudding

December 12th — By now you see

By now you see,
That Christmas tree,
Is looking full,
All underneath,
***
Presents for her,
And for him as well,
Presents for them,
This year is year will be swell,
***
So, take a moment to look,
Just a moment to peek,
Do you think on Christmas eve,
You'll be able to sleep?

December 13th — Winter Philosophy

It's during these,
Dark cold days,
I remember a philosophy,
To keep in mind,
"Don't waste this time,
Wishing away,
These winter days,
Just to spend,
Your future months,
Wishing you could,
relive them just once."

December 14th — Christmas Coco

Grab yourself a tall mug,
Get a bag of marshmallows,
Heat a pan of milk,
Take three heaps of chocolate,
Pour it all in one,
Now take a sip,
Have a seat,
And wait for Christmas to come.

December 15th — Jack Frost

Hi Mr Jack Frost,
Welcome in again,
Take up a seat,
And let it snow,
Icicles will grow,
steel will groan,
But pretty please,
Leave it outside,
Of our homes.

December 16th — Snow Man

There once was a snowman,
Who was such a glum man,
That had no nose to show,
Along came a Santa,
Who stopped alongside him,
And gave the snowman a nose.

December 17th — Riddle 3

I have many names,
From frosty to Olaf,
I am usually white,
Or whatever rubs off,
You can give me a nose,
Or choose to not,
My coal coat buttons,
Always fall off.

What am I?

I am a Snowman

December 19th — Thought to The Less Fortunate

Through the celebrations,
And through all the cheer,
Let's just spend a moment,
And give a thought to those not here,
To those less well off,
And to those who suffer,
at this time of year.

December 20th — Nativity

All though we may not all believe it,
The story still persists,
Let's remember the nativity.
***
It is said that long time ago,
Bethlehem was host to the host,
Can you hear the nativity?
***
We are told that Jesus was born,
In a stable on Christmas Day,
Do you feel the nativity?
***
Now we may not all believe it,
And we may not all follow it,
But please don't forget the nativity.

December 21st — My Christmas Wish to a Special Someone

I know you are not with me,
And there are miles between us,
But do not frown,
And do not fret,
In just over a week,
We will be back together yet.
***

Lots of love, xxx

December 22nd — Christmas is Coming

Times a ticking,
Days are passing,
People dance all night long,
Christmas is coming,
Closer by the hour,
Families come together,
And we all get along.

December 23rd — Oh Christmas Tree

Oh Christmas tree,
That glitters so bright,
With tempting gifts,
And glowing lights,
Just two days left,
'till I get at you,
And rip open my gifts,
From underneath you.

December 24th — Christmas Eve

As you close your eyes tonight,
And keep those lids shut so tight,
When you make that one last wish,
For a gift from old St Nick,
Let me just sprinkle,
This bit of cheer,
And wish,
Your Christmas wish comes true this year.
***

Merry Christmas from CreativelyBecomeIndiffernet

December 25th — Merry Christmas

Christmastide is here again,
And may I extend good greetings,
To foe and friend,
Christmas is for family,
For loved ones and all,
Not for fighting, hating or war.

Merry Christmas to all and to all a good night.

December 25th — Christmas Wishes

It's time,
We have counted down,
Our calendars are finished,
And now that day is here,
May all your wishes be granted,
And may you have an amazing Christmas this year.

December 25th — Merry Christmas

Merry Christmas,
From me to you,
Enjoy the presents,
And the food,
Greet your family,
And hug your friends.

December 25th — Christmas Thank You

This has been my third year,
My third Christmas,
And I'm still here,
Thank you for reading,
Thank you for following,
Thank you for commenting,
Thank you for everything,
Now for the countdown to the new year.

Christmas Countdown 2015

Christmas 2015 marked the fourth countdown. The fourth year into a project that was not supposed to outlive university. If you had told me in 2012 that Creatively Become Indifferent would be so successful I would have laughed. By this point though, life had begun to get busy...

December 1st — Let the Countdown Begin

Merry Christmas all,
Another year is here,
The Christmas spirit,
And Festive cheer,
Will flow out to all,
As we count down to Christmas,
For this blog's fourth year.

December 2^{ns} — Get Christmas Started

Christmas adverts in full swing,
Trees in full bling,
Carolers in full sing,
So let's deck the halls,
And decorate the walls,
In time for the festive cheer.

December 3rd — Three Weeks to Go

It's only the third,
With three weeks to go,
As of tomorrow.

So look outside,
And watch it snow,
And enjoy the tree weeks to go.

December 4th — The Christmas Tree Melody

From the ground up,
My tree is always,
A sight to see.
***
There is the tinsel,
Wrapped round,
With the bobbles,
Poking through,
Some of glass,
Some ceramic,
And some only held together by glue.
***
But half way up,
There is one sight to see,
The handmade decoration,
Made when I was three.
***
Mum insisted it was kept,
But you see,
I think it looks sloppy,
And "not like me",
But tradition is tradition,
And now it hangs firm,
Below the other pieces of tinsel
And fir,
***
At the top sits a fairy,
A star was too mainstream,

And up underneath her,
One of the fairy lights gleam,
It glistens through her dress,
For all to see,
But it is probably most uncomfortable,
For that little fairy.

December 5th — Underneath the Tree

There is only a small pile,
Underneath the tree,
Most of them bought,
And wrapped by me,
Those are the ones,
Waiting for delivery,
And soon to be replaced,
By the presents meant for me.

December 6th — The Pet Owners Ballad

All the pet owner will agree,
This time of year,
Is not easy.
***
If it's cats you must watch,
Then the baubles might get knocked,
If it is dogs that you keep,
Then it's the disappearing presents you might seek,
But either way,
The worst of all,
The cat-astrophic loss,
Of the Christmas tree.

December 7th — Snow White

Snow White,
Snow bright,
Fall outside my house tonight.

Snow men,
Stand strong,
While the winter marches on.

December 8th — Memories of Long Ago

The smell of Christmas,
We all know,
It jingles memories,
Of times long ago,
It brings thoughts of presents,
And of snow,
Of the presents we got,
And the Christmas tree glow,
It also makes new memories,
That stay as we grow,
And will remind us of this Christmas,
When it is long ago.

December 9th — Hidden Message from Me

Read between the lines,
Understand what you see,
Don't assume it's all written,
On here for you by me,
Learn to look again,
Perhaps you will see something,
Here that wasn't there before.
***
There are things in this world,
Hidden from view,
Eight visit each year.
***
Right around Christmas,
Exactly their speed,
Does anyone know.
***
Night is their cover,
Over the world,
Santa calling,
Each of the herd,
During the night.
***
Read between the lines,
Everyone can see,
I have hidden a name,
Not unknown to you,
Did you spot the trick?
Each stanza a word,

Each sentence a letter,
Read again what do you see?

December 10th — International Human Rights Day

From Drippy the Raindrop,
To Frosty the Snowman,
From the water cycle,
The winter in the slums,
From pressure systems,
To mountain snow,
A geography teacher's job,
Is a continuing show.

December 11th — Ice Cold Haiku

Snow is cold as ice,
White and pure like fresh boiled rice,
And most falls at night,

December 12th — Jingle Bells

There are chestnuts roasting by open fires,
And jingle bells being rung,
So let's have a jolly Christmas,
And spread the fun.

December 13th — One Day Closer

It's one day closer,
One day nearer,
St. Nicholas will visit,
And bring his reindeer,
They will drag his sleigh here,
From the artic.

December 14th — *Special Snow Flake*

Somewhere out there,
Not too far away,
Our hears are calling,
Where we need to be.

Find that someone,
Let them know their loved,
And never forget,
Know you are loved,
Each and every day.

December 15th — Ten Days

Ten days to go,
How the present pile grows,
What did you wish for,
Is it under the tree,
Not long to wait,
To find out and see.

December 16th — Channel Hopping

Getting ready for the Christmas cheer,
With Doctor Who and Strictly here,
Looking out for Christmas specials,
Such as Emmerdale, extenders and casualty,
Comedy, cheer and family fun,
Broken by channel hopping to find what's on.

December 17th — Shameless Branding Plug

Here's a shameless branding plug,
On the final days before gifts are given,
Think smartwatch think Samsung,
Think TV then think Sony,
Think headphones it's Beats,
Think underwear it has to be Clonezone,
And finally holidays think QE2 with Cunard.

December 18th — The Scrooge Among Us

There is always one,
At this time of year,
That takes the fun,
And steals the cheer,
Who hates the laughter,
And dislikes the joy,
Well ignore them I say,
And have a happier day.

December 19th — Christmas Cheer

Christmas comes but once a year,
And with it comes the Christmas cheer.
Let's all meet and be jolly,
Let get out the Christmas holly.
Dust off the Christmas tree,
And get out the Christmas CD.
Meet those long lost friends,
And hope the cheer never ends.

December 20th — A Few Things to Do

Hold hands and sing,
Carols of the days gone,
And prophesies of times to come.
***
Kiss under the mistletoe,
And don't tell Santa you've been naughty,
While we gather round the tree.
***
Break out the drink,
And take a drink to the times,
With the friends and family you don't often see.
***
These are a few,
Of the things to do,
At Christmas time.

December 21st — *Alliteration All Around*

Santa shifts sacks while,
Rudolf rides right up front.
Snowmen stand silent where,
Winter washes white.
Couples cuddle cutely while,
Winds whistle weakly.
Save some sherry,
Have hearty hours,
Love life loud and,
Spread some cheer for me.

December 22nd — Gift a Smile

Christmas is a time for joy,
A time of giving,
And a time of receiving.
***
Remember to give love,
not just gifts,
And enjoy the receiving.
***
Life is too short,
Not to love,
Or share it with others.
***
Give a cuddle to those in need,
And watch the smiles,
Start to spread.

December 23rd — Last Minute Shop

Turkey, got it,
Milk, yep that to,
We all know the sound,
Of the last minute shop,
You know there is more,
But you just want to stop,
And when you are done,
You know there will be,
Someone or something,
You have forgot,
And you will be back,
For a last, last minute shop.

December 24th — Build-up to Christmas

Well here we are again,
The eve of the celebration,
Let's look back at the year,
And look forward to a new one.
Today is the quiet before the storm,
Opening presents and visit the family,
Thank those for their gifts,
And thank those for their presence,
But for now there is time to rest,
And build up to the big day.

December 25th — Merry Christmas

Merry Christmas,
My many readers,
May you get what you want,
May your lunch be delicious,
May you all have a Merry Christmas.

December 25th — Spread the Cheer

Happy Christmas, One and all,
Young and old, Gay or straight,
Single or married, Christian or Atheist,
This time should not be about defining people,
It's about bringing people together,
So find someone random,
And spread the cheer,
Just wish them a Merry Christmas,
And a happy new year.

December 25th — Ode to Christmas Dinner

Oh to the meal,
To the dinner,
To all you at this table,
Never has a time,
Reminded me so,
Of what family is.
Here's to the food we are about to eat,
The carrots and broccoli and sprouts,
Here's to the company,
The friends and the family.
Never this year,
Have I seen a meal so delicious,
And never for a year,
Will I see it again.

December 25th — Merry Christmas Fiancé

You may not be here,
And may not see me,
But Merry Christmas,
And don't worry,
There is still a present for you,
Under the tree.
I love you,
My darling fiancé.

New Year Countdown 2015

After the lack of a New Year Countdown in 2014 a couple of my avid were insistent that I write a new year countdown. The muses were not on my side while I wrote, due to the lack of interest in 2013. So, as a compromise, there were two poems written. Thus giving birth to the most pointless section of this book.

December 27th — When All's Said and Done

It's that time of the year,
Where we meet family,
Get your friends round,
Celebrate the year been,
The year to come,
Wait for the bells,
And laugh,
When all's said and done.

December 30th — One Day More

One Day More,
Another day towards another year,
This never ending road to 2016,
This year seems to be running out of time,
Counting down with each chime,
One Day More.

Christmas Countdown 2016

Then there was 2016... As you read through these poems you may notice something, they are a collection of other years' poems. 2016, being the fifth year, became first attempt to end the countdown, thus it was a compendium of the top ranking poems from the previous four years. The sad thing is, I cannot remember if there are any new poems at all in 2016. Note, no New Year Countdown.

Creatively Become Indifferent was also wrapped up in 2016. Having run from the London Olympics in 2012, May 2016 felt like the right time to end it. The goal of Creatively Become Indifferent was to prove a rather rude educational psychologist wrong following an identification as dyslexic. On that fateful day I was asked, "what do you want to do with your life". Apparently, "writing", was not the answer they were expecting, and was met with a, "you may want to think about something else".

The reason for ending Creatively Become Indifferent was to focus on Poetry as an artform. While I love writing short stories, and even had/have a Sci-Fi novel in the works, poetry was short form enough to fit around my life and was the most popular form of writing I worked on. So to create this focus, Pesky Poetry™ was brought to life.

December 1st — Welcome to December

Where has this year gone,
Come again is another December,
Gone now is the November.
***
Year end is soon to come,
And with this Christmas cheer,
So, here's to the future, Christmas, and New Year.
***
Without further ado,
Let's start December as we should,
With a Christmas calendar countdown.

December 2nd — Puzzle Number One: Riddle Me This

What am I in the morning?
But not in the night,
I make the cocks crow,
And the first morning light,
I am only once a day,
Every day of the year,
I get earlier in the summer,
Later in the fall,
And I am well known,
For showing the new day to all.

December 3rd — Jack Frost

There's a nip in the air,
And some ice over there,
The windows are foggy,
And the roads are all slippy,
I guess you could say,
Jack Frost has been busy,
***
He's been making the cold,
And you never know,
In the night,
It might snow,
So wrap up warm,
when you go out,
All together now,
"Let it snow, let it snow, let it snow!"

December 4th — Keep Me Warm

The cold is back this year,
And I have you here,
Stay with me the night,
Keep me warm from the cold.
***
Please stay with me,
And never leave me,
Stay with me this winter,
Stay with me forever.
***
Please don't just be a Christmas dream,
Say you will never leave me,
Kiss me and take me tonight,
And cuddle with me through the night.
***
I will keep you warm,
And never let the cold get you,
If you will just be mine,
I will never leave to be lonely.

December 5th — Friends

Friends are what make life fun,
They mix it up and get it done,
Without friends life would be dull,
And life would hit a bit of a lull,
So in this season of goodwill,
Let's share our thanks to good friends,
And hope the friendship never ends.

December 6th — *Sing Sweet Melodies*

Sing sweet melodies of Christmas times,
Let's all remember last year,
And the Christmas we have got here,
***
Sing sweet melodies of mulled wine,
And decorating halls,
For the holidays time.
***
Sing sweet melodies of friends,
And of the times,
Let's hope it never ends.
***
Sing sweet melodies of all the fun,
That this year brung,
Just because we can.

December 7th — Snow Day

Hip Hip Hooray,
It's a snow day.
Gone is the rain,
Back is the snow games.
Snow balls are readied,
For the winter wars.
Out are the gritters,
Clearing the roads.
So peaceful and calm,
The countryside looks,
On this, a beautiful snow day.

December 8th — Snow Globe

Shake that snow globe,
Give it a wish,
Let old saint nick,
Know what's on your list,
***
Don't miss that mistletoe,
Come on give me a kiss,
You never know,
You could be my wish.

December 9th — Cold Christmas Riddle

I can be made,
And unmade,
I can be one among many,
Or grouped to form something,
***

Some use me,
As a weapon,
In the games they play.
***

With a shovel,
And someone who knows,
I make a dome,
For Eskimos.
***

With some coal,
A scarf, a hat,
And some magic,
I form a friend.
***

What am I?

December 10th — *International Human Rights Day*

Every so often,
We just need to pause,
Think of others,
As we think of ourselves.
***

Everyone is someone,
A someone with dreams,
With aspirations,
And importantly with feelings.
***

Today gives us chance,
To reflect on those,
Who don't have what they need,
And get what they don't deserve.
***

This year for International Human Rights day,
Spread some cheer,
And share a smile,
A little thing could make a big difference.

December 11th — Happy Holidays

Happy holidays,
One and all,
Let the joy ring out,
Leave the hate behind,
Yesterday is history,
Look to tomorrow.
***

Remember this is the season,
Everyone should smile,
Extend the hand of friendship,
For you are only here for a short while.

December 12th — Halfway There

We're halfway there,
Trees have been decorated,
Hats and scarfs out for a while,
The New Year feels closer,
Than at any time,
Parties have been planned,
And gift preparation is in full swing,
Christmas carols are being sung,
The season has well and truly begun.

December 13th — Christmas Jingle

Have you got your Christmas turkey,
Fa la la la la, la la la la.
All the stuffing and the trimming,
Fa la la la la, la la la la.
*

It's all sitting in the freezer.
Fa la la, la la la, la la la.
Waiting for the Christmas dinner.
Fa la la la la, la la la la.
*

Kids excited for the presents,
Fa la la la la, la la la la.
And everyone has gifts to share,
Fa la la la la, la la la la.
*

Let's all sing in joy together,
Fa la la la la, la la la la.
And forget about the weather,
Fa la la la la, la la la la.

December 14th — Monkey Day

Hay hay todays a good day,
Welcome to the day,
Where monkey business is ok,
December the 14th,
Is Monkey Day.
***

Get out of the house,
And play in the snow,
Or if there is none,
Just have some fun,
For today is the one day a year,
It ok to make light and merry,
And be a little monkey.

December 15th — Ten Days to Go

Ten days to go,
And by now you all know,
Christmas is coming close,
And so is the snow,
In comes the cold,
Out comes the coal,
As the cold takes its toll.
***

Thermoses are filled,
Drinks are no longer chilled,
And the garden no longer has a rose,
But we wait in delight,
For that one starry night,
With only ten days to go.

December 16th — *Santa Claus*

Santa Claus even if not here,
Brings joy to kids,
Every Year,
***

With his reindeer and sled,
And shiny bald head,
He comes out each year,
***

In supermarkets and stalls,
And even school halls,
His sits and waits this year,
***

He'll soon be on his way,
After stalking his sleigh,
And Christmas Eve is here.

December 17th — Christmas Plans

There are snowmen,
With snow balls,
Rudolf calls,
And we deck the halls.
***

We shake hands,
Make Christmas Plans,
Sing Psalms,
And meet our grans,
***

While I write poetry,
We sing happily,
Smile profusely,
Living our Christmas plans.

December 18th — Christmas to Me

There are the Christmas tunes,
There is a turkey in the oven,
There's a smile on the faces,
A laugh coming from the table,
There are the lights on the tree,
And let's not forget the company,
This is what Christmas means to me.
***
People all around the world feel as one,
All link arms together and thank everyone,
Remember the hardships of the past,
And the hardships to come,
But not focus of the hard times,
But look forward to the fun,
This is what I dream Christmas to be.

December 19th — Christmas Riddle 3

Someone in your chimney,
After the kids have gone to bed,
Night comes and he arrives,
While the kids rest their heads,
***
He likes milk,
And warm cookies,
Sat by the fire,
While he leaves goodies by the tree,
For the kids to admire,
So who is he?

December 20th — Happy Hanukkah

It's Hanukkah,
And I know what I wanna da'
It's a time for remembrance,
It's a time for enlightenment.
***
Even if you don't observe it,
We have all heard it,
And so I raise this to everyone,
Have a happy Hanukkah.

December 21st — *Solstice*

The solstice marks the darkest day,
And today, of the darkest year,
Let's hold a hope,
Next year will be better,
But don't bet on it.

December 22nd — Here's to Christmas

Here's to the tree,
Standing so proudly,
Decorated in all the fineries,
***
Here's to the gifts,
All stacked neatly,
Just waiting for Sunday,
***
Here's to the parents,
Running off their feet,
Finding gifts for the kids,
***
And here's to the kids,
All excited and cheery,
Waiting for Santa's visit.

December 23rd — Christmas Week

So here we are,
It's that week,
Christmas is near,
And the weather is bleak.

But although the weather is bleak,
And there is no snow on the ground,
Let's all remember the family we have,
And give a thought to those around.

Forget family feuds,
And let the past go,
Remember family are family,
No matter what they do.

December 24th — Christmas Eve

Come all ye faithful,
Have a drink and laugh with us,
Right now is the night,
In come the cheers,
So tomorrow will bring the joy,
Tots with toys full of noise,
Mothers and fathers searching for batteries,
And not a soul should feel sad,
Singers of carols will fill the air.
***
Everyone everywhere,
Ventures out to the family houses,
Each to greet and wish a merry Christmas.

December 25th — Merry Christmas

Merry Christmas one and all,
Welcome to the new day,
Let's us toast to the turkey,
And give thanks for the gifts.
***
Let's give thanks to the people who cooked the meal,
And let us not forget the dishes.
We will all be tired come tonight,
So let's enjoy the day while its light.
***
Christmas wouldn't be Christmas,
Without the friends and family,
And of course to me that includes you,
Thank you for reading, Merry Christmas to you,
***
Now get back to your Christmas,
And enjoy your day,
Join me tomorrow,
Until New Year's Day.

Christmas Countdown 2018

2017, where is 2017? Oh, that was the year that never was. 2016 was supposed to be the last year of the Christmas Countdown. As life got busier, and readership of Pesky Poetry didn't pick up, it was almost curtains for the whole thing. One of the unanticipated consequences of spinning up Pesky Poetry, and archiving Creatively Become Indifferent, was that followers would not jump over to Pesky Poetry. Makes sense though. Over 90% of readers on Pesky Poetry find the site or return to the site rather than follow via email or the site. But that is expected, there is no real FOMO to poetry and it is often situational.

So why did 2018 become a thing? On the 3rd of December 2017 one of my avid followers reached out to ask why I had missed the 1st and 2nd. When I responded that the Christmas Countdown was over, they sent a long message about how they like the poetry advent calendar and it was one of the main reasons for following. We chatted a bit, and I said that it was too late for 2017 but I promised a full countdown for 2018. There are some duplicate poems in here from previous years, either gaps to fill or updating old poems when they were posted in 2018.

November 30th — Christmas Countdown

It's that time again,
To ring it in,
Spread the cheer,
And mark the end of the year.
***
Get your elf shoes on,
The tree out,
Dust off the lights,
And get excited.
***
Return to here,
On December the 1st,
For a daily poem,
Like a chocolate in a calendar.

December 1st — The First Chocolate

It's that first crisp morning,
When you sneak out of bed,
Head down the stairs,
Grab your calendar,
And hear that door tear,
Underneath is that sweetest of treats,
The first seasons chocolate,
There for you to eat.

December 2nd — Christmas Tree

A
Tree
Has many
Levels to it
Some are lit
Some are not
Some with tinsel
Some with baubles
Some nothing on at all
But
We can all
Agree
Presents should be underneath it

December 3rd — Hot Chocolate

Winter isn't winter,
Without a nice hot drink,
A large vat of something,
Sweet and soothing,
Topped off with mint,
And mallows too,
To keep you warm,
From your hat to your shoes.

December 4th — Christmas Wish List

I've made my list,
I've checked it twice,
I know I've been not naughty,
But nice.
***

You are on my list,
But under which heading,
Will it be hell or heaven?

December 5th — Will You Get the Coal

Naughty or nice,
Once or twice,
Throughout the year,
Or once a cold night,
What will it be,
The gift or the coal,
For you this year,
Only Santa will know.

December 6th — Decorate That Tree

Get the boxes out,
Blow off the dust,
Clean out the lights,
Buff the tinsel up,
Open the tree,
Argue about baubles,
And who does the fairy,
Or is it a star,
Who give a care,
By the end of today,
Let's just have one up anyway.

December 7th — Holiday Countdown

Whether it's the kids, Or the adults,
By now one things in sight,
The last day of work,
With the first off night.
We count down the days,
To the holiday off,
And before we know it,
We'll all be off.

December 8th — Christmas Shop

Chop Chop,
Time to shop,
Christmas is on the way,
***
Quick Quick,
Get your pick,
For the holiday,
***
Run Run,
Get it done,
Don't let it slip away.

December 9th — Happy Hanukkah

It's Hanukkah,
And I know what I wanna da'
It's a time for remembrance,
It's a time for enlightenment.
***
Even if you don't observe it,
We have all heard it,
And so I raise this to everyone,
Have a happy Hanukkah.

December 10th — That's a Wrap

Pompoms and ribbons and bows and tape,
The things you need to make the shape,
Wrap the box in shiny paper,
Tie it shut with a little taper,
Tape it down and put it away,
To be ripped open another day.

December 11th — Friends

Friends are what make life fun,
They mix it up and get it done,
Without friends life would be dull,
And life would hit a bit of a lull,
So in this season of goodwill,
Let's share our thanks to good friends,
And hope the friendship never ends.

December 12th — Christmas Round the World

The Aussies have their barbecues,
The Eskimos build their igloos,
The Scots grab their sleds,
And the bears go to bed.
***

Each corner of the earth,
Has its own ways to go,
Whether that's sunny,
Or temperatures sub-zero.
***

One thing we all share,
Is spreading cheer,
And sharing what we have,
With those who do not.

December 13th — Christmas Jingle

Have you got your Christmas turkey,
Fa la la la la, la la la la.
All the stuffing and the trimming,
Fa la la la la, la la la la.

*

It's all sitting in the freezer.
Fa la la, la la la, la la la.
Waiting for the Christmas dinner.
Fa la la la la, la la la la.

*

Kids excited for the presents,
Fa la la la la, la la la la.
And everyone has gifts to share,
Fa la la la la, la la la la.

*

Lets all sing in joy together,
Fa la la la la, la la la la.
And forget about the weather,
Fa la la la la, la la la la.

December 14th — Monkey Day

Hay hay todays a good day,
Welcome to the day,
Where monkey business is ok,
December the 14th,
Is Monkey Day.
***

get out of the house,
And play in the snow,
Or if there is none,
Just have some fun,
For today is the one day a year,
It ok to make light and merry,
And be a little monkey.

December 15th — Ten Days to Go

Ten days to go,
And by now you all know,
Christmas is close,
And so is the snow,
In comes the cold,
Out comes the coal,
As the cold takes its toll.
***
Thermoses are filled,
Drinks are no longer chilled,
And the garden no longer has a rose,
But we wait in delight,
For that one starry night,
With only ten days to go.

December 16th — Santa Claus

Santa Claus even if not here,
Brings joy to kids,
Every Year,
***

With his reindeer and sled,
And shiny bald head,
He comes and spreads cheer,
***

In supermarkets and stalls,
And even school halls,
His sits and waits this year,
***

He'll soon be on his way,
After stocking his sleigh,
And Christmas Eve is here.

December 18th — Present for You

Roses are red,
Violets are blue,
There's something under the tree,
Just for you.
***
Tulips are black,
Pansies are blue,
Christmas is nothing,
When I'm not with you.

December 19th — Snow Men

There are snow men,
With snow balls,
Rudolf calls,
And we deck the halls.

We shake hands,
And make plans,
Sing psalms,
And we meet our grans.

I write poems,
Clap my hands,
Smile at my plans,
And thank you my fans.

December 20th — Knocking at The Door

Hear that knocking at the door,
You recognize it from long before,
It that long lost family member,
Who only shows at Christmas.
***

Who's that now at the door,
A knocking unlike before,
Could it be the next-door friend,
Spreading cheer at Christmas.
***

There sounds a sharp coughing,
Preluding another knocking,
Who's that at the door,
Another guest for Christmas.
***

Now with all and sundry here,
You can drink Christmas cheer,
And sing in the bells,
For here's to another Christmas.

December 21ˢᵗ — *Happy Solstice*

21st is here,
And that only means one thing,
The darkest day of the year.
In history we would have freed,
The sun not returning,
Or the forest not being here.
Now we can appreciate,
The beauty of it all,
Now it is scientifically clear.
The sun will rise,
The trees will grow,
And winter will be here.

December 22nd — Cold of Snow

The ground turns hard,
The sky turns grey,
The world becomes cold,
As we near the end of the day.
***
The wind begins to howl,
The night begins to clear,
Giving way to the white,
Of Christmas Cheer.
***
The children are out playing,
On the temporary play turf,
Making the most of it,
Before it goes for another year.

December 23rd — Last Advent Sunday

Here we are,
The last Sunday of advent,
Where Christians remember,
Joseph, Mary and the donkey who bore her.
***
Here we are,
The Sunday before Christmas,
Where everyone remembers,
The act of gift giving and gift receiving.
***
Here we are,
The last week of the year,
You don't have to be a Christian,

December 24th — To appreciate the humanity of advent.
Advent Candles

My first candle was for Hope,
The hope for the year to come,
The hope for everyone,
A reminder of things to come,
And things that could have been.
***
The second candle was for Peace,
Not just at home with family,
But with everyone around the world,
A reminder that Peace,
Is not just a worldwide or home-based problem.
***
Last week's candle was for Joy,
The sense we feel around friends,
When we have successes,
A reminder of the positive in the world,
Even when the world can look bleak.
***
Today I light the last candle,
The candle for Love,
To me it is a reminder,
Not to forget the loved ones I've lost,
And the loved ones I have.
***
You don't have to be a Christian,
To light a candle at this time of year.
Light is a symbol universally,

No matter your faith or fear.
Today I light my candle for Love,
And watch Hope, Peace and Joy glow.
My candles light a path for me,
Through the dark part of my year.
Through loss of loved ones,
These candles will help me see my way.

December 24th — Sweet Old Saint Nic

He's climbing in your window,
Laying your presents out,
Bringing joy to your house,
And not waking your kids up,
He's made his list,
And he has checked it twice,
He knows who is naughty,
And who has been nice,
Here comes Saint Nic,
All quiet and sweet,
Sneaking around,
While everyone sleeps.

December 25th — Christmas Thanks

Thank you all,
For another year,
Of reading my attempt,
To spread Christmas cheer,
***
The next week,
Will be New Year,
So please keep reading,
The last countdown here.
***
All that's left,
Is for me to say,
Merry Christmas to you,
Happy New Year on the way.

December 25th — Turkey and Wine

Christmas time,
Turkey and Wine,
Parents mumbling Christmas rhymes.
There cake in the fridge,
Queen's speech on the news,
Time to rejoice all the good we can do,
It's a time for drinking,
A time for overeating,
A time for napping,
off all the food we have eaten.

New Year Countdown 2018

I don't really know what to say here. 2018 included a New Year Countdown because I was asked nicely, but I only wrote three poems. By a long way, the 2018 Christmas Countdown was a great success with that success I decided to take future years much more seriously.

December 27th — Turkey Again! Again!

Why do we do this every year,
We overdo it on Christmas cheer,
And manage to cook more bird than we need,
So you end up with sandwiches, curries and all things turkey,
Somehow you find ways,
You've never done before,
To use the meat of the oversized bird,
Without letting any go to waste.

December 29th — What's That Over The Hill?

What's that coming over the hill?
Is it Easter? Could it be Easter?
When's too early for shops to stock?
Eggs for Easter? For Easter.
Why have you read a poem in December?
About Easter? Easter!

December 30th — Annual Thank You

It's become tradition,
To write a thank you to all my readers,
Without you I'd be writing for nothing.
***

Thank you for your Likes and Follows,
They are very appreciated,
And make this project worthwhile.
***

This year has been amazing,
More than 800 visitors, 1100 views, 170 likes,
All thanks to you.
***

So here's to 2019,
A scary thought if you ask me,
For a 3 year project started in 2012.

Christmas Countdown 2019

The last year of the 2010s so much potential, but who could have known what 2020 would bring? Before the mess that was the early 2020s this countdown was the most successful. All new poems and even a whole new countdown. Avoiding the personal religious discission, 2019 saw the creation of an Advent Countdown, but we will get to that in the next chapter.

December 1ˢᵗ — The Countdown Has Begun

Hear me, hear me,
One and all.
Christmas is coming,
The countdown in running.
A poem a day,
Is on the way.
So stay tuned to me,
For you will see,
The Christmas Countdown by Pesky Poetry.

December 1st — Advent Sunday

Day number one,
Of the Christmas Countdown,
Another year draws to a close,
Celebrate the Advent with me,
While the winter wind blows.
***

Each day to Christmas,
Then on to new year,
A poem will be published,
Chronicling the journey there,
***

While Advent Sunday,
Falls on the first,
May this December be fun,
Right through to January.

December 2nd — Christmas Card

Christmas comes but once a year,
Helping people remember their,
Roots and where they come from.
Instead of fighting and hating,
Share love and go skating,
Trim the turkey and share in drinking.
Merry singers stand on corners,
Announcing their choral warmers,
Sharing joy and love to walkers.

Come and join the cheer with me,
And dance around the Christmas tree,
Rejoice for all the world to see,
Denouncing hate and animosity.

December 3rd — They've Defrosted Bublé

It's a sure sign Christmas has come,
As the great singer wakes,
From his slumber down under,
And shares a song with everyone.
***

A new album and some cheer,
Maybe a sweet jungle bells,
Or something more swing,
We all recognise his deep voice.
***

So let's acknowledged,
They've defrosted Bublé,
And that it must be,
Close to Christmas.

December 4th — Christmas Shop Fronts

Shops get all dressed up,
At this time of year,
To share and be known,
The Christmas Cheer.
***

Windows with lights round,
And deer on the ground,
Santa sat in the back,
Next to a present
***

Frosty sells another toy,
For a stocking of a girl or boy,
The shops flow with Christmas joy,
At this time of year.

December 5th — It's Christmas Haiku

Now That It's Christmas,
Show love and peace to all men,
And let your love shine.

Now That It's Christmas,
Show love and peace to all men,
In God's name Amen.

December 6ᵗʰ — They're Coming

Brace yourself,
For they are coming.
Every year,
They take to huffing.
No smiles,
Will be on their face.
No cheer,
Will they share today.
Bah Humbug,
They will all oblige.
Scrooges!
Have come so let's hide.

December 7th — Christmas Card from Afar

In this time of electronic communication,
There is still one postage that gets us sending,
Cards are a perfect way to say,
Merry Christmas to you on this day.
***

Cards are sent from all corners of the world,
Where Christmas is a barbecue down by the reef,
Followed by something cooling and sweet,
Or it could mean snowmen in the garden.
***

Within that pile of letters and circulars,
It is nice to see a card shaped bill,
One that on opening will bring you a thrill,
A Merry Christmas from someone who remembers you still.

December 8th — Christmas Shopping

Nothing beats the thrill,
Of walking under the warm draft,
Entering a highstreet shop,
From the cold step.
***
Finding things for others,
Toys, food and drink,
Knowing they will get opened,
After Christmas eve.
***
Picking stocking fillers,
And kids new toys,
Stuff to play with,
For girls and boys.
***
But after the buying,
Comes the wrapping,
The next job needing done,
on the big Christmas list.

December 9th — Robin

Roaming over the land,
Over the bushes in your garden,
Bobbing between post to post,
It's a symbol of the time of year,
Nothing says winter like a robin.

December 10th — Christmas Tree

A stoic symbol to the life of the forest,
Something we aim to preserve,
A way of caring for mother nature,
And the other plants and animals of this earth.
***
Now a symbol of want and greed,
Put up to shade our presents,
We use it as a giant decoration,
A multi coloured shining tree.
***
Please use this time of year,
To remember the animals and plants,
Recycle reuse and dispose of responsibly,
Just like our ancestors Christmas tree plans.

December 11th — *Who Politicised Christmas*

Who the hell politicised Christmas,
A time that supposed to be fun,
No one wants to think about politics,
When they are doing the Christmas run,
But given the importance of this vote,
Please don't forget to go out,
And cast you wishes whatever they may be,
Tomorrow when the vote comes about.

December 12th — Cute Tree Haiku

Red light, Green Light, Blue,
This tree is flashing for you,
Doesn't it look cute?

December 13th — Christmas Movies

Whether it's the Muppets or Jack Skellington,
Or the Hog Father followed by Scrooge,
Or some holiday tale of the days that were good.
***
Christmas movies fill the airwaves,
Bringing joy and Christmas excitement,
To adults and children both young and old.
***
Grab the TV guide from the pile,
Give a quick flip through the file,
Find a movie to watch while,
You countdown to Christmas day.

December 14th — Monkey Day

Let's show some love,
This Christmas time,
To all things simian.
***
Out cousins here,
On this planet green,
On the life tree.
***
Thank you Millikin & Sorrow,
For this day to think,
About our furry brothers.

December 15th — Mistletoe

My favourite part of this time of year,
Is sitting here with a beer,
Waiting patiently for you here,
To meet me under the white berries there.
***

Below the mistletoe up there,
I'll wait to share a kiss right here,
Just sitting here with my beer,
To love you at this time of year.

December 16th — Snowman

Soundless as it falls,
Nothing is shown until it thaws,
Ominous in its covering,
Winter sight across the land,
Mountains white in the distance,
And perfect for making,
None other than a snowman.

December 17th — Morning Frost

Crunch Crunch,
The ground beneath my feet,
Crunch Crunch,
The grass frozen to peat,
Crunch Crunch,
The frozen washed sheets,
Crunch Crunch,
The absolute void of heat,
Of the cold morning frost.

December 18th — One Week To Go

There's one week to go,
Until the big day,
And in that time,
There is a lot to do.
***
The schools must finish,
With hyper kids,
Leaving for the holidays,
And dreaming of their presents.
***
And don't Forget,
That last little bit,
Of wrapping to do,
For under the tree.
***
That and the turkey,
You need to get,
From the store,
That is getting hectic.
***
But in that time,
Remember to enjoy,
Some of the cheer,
And maybe some wine.

December 19th — Jingle Bells Haiku

Jingle bells to you,
To your own and everyone,
Wherever you are.

December 19th — Christmas Lights

Twinkle Twinkle Christmas lights,
Shine down you joy here tonight,
Spread the happiness you bring,
Keep everyone smiling,
Twinkle Twinkle Christmas lights,
How I love you at night.

December 20th — Christmas Travel

We get up early,
And warm the car,
Pack the gifts,
To travel far,
Grab a bite,
And grab a tea,
We'll be on our way.

December 21ˢᵗ — Darkest Time

Winter Solstice,
Comes over us,
Making the world dark.
***
But tomorrow will be light,
And shorter will be the night,
bringing back the warmth.
***
Although today is dark,
Look to tomorrow,
As the start of a brighter time.

December 22nd — Yule Log

Yuletide wishes to all of you,
May the Yuletide bring something new.
Keep the Yule log burning in the hearth,
And a pound of love in your heart.
Let all and sunder know you care,
And that you will always be there.
So happy Yuletide to you and yours,
Wrap up warm and don't let Christmas pass in a blur.

December 23rd — Reindeer

Right around the corner,
Each child is wearing,
In will come Santa Clause,
No sound he will be making,
Down on the roof,
Each house he will visit,
Ever quiet and still,
Reindeer silent on hoof.

December 24th — Get Excited

There are traditions to uphold,
And new ones to make,
A Christmas tea to be had,
And cakes to be baked,
Movies to watch,
And board games to be played,
And that one tradition,
We all insist has just been made.
***
But after the excitement,
It's time to sleep,
Before he sees you,
When he creeps,
And drops down the chimney,
With sooty foot,
To leave the presents,
Where the tree is stood.
***
Sleep well in the thought,
That Santa will come,
His gifts will bring joy,
To everyone,
And make sure to leave,
One thing out for he,
A drink of milk or maybe some brandy.

December 25th — Merry Christmas

As you sit warm,
In your PJs,
Eyeing up your presents.
***
Have a happy Christmas,
And spread the love,
At this time of sharing.
***
We all love a good gift,
Or hidden surprise,
And treat under the tree.
***
So celebrate everyone,
Show your heart,
And hug your family.
***
Merry Christmas to you,
From the PeskyPoet.

December 25th — Christmas Countdown 2020

It's come and gone,
For another year,
The presents are open,
And so is the beer,
Now all that's left,
Is to say,
365 days left,
Till the next Christmas Day.

Advent Countdown 2019

This was the first of the Advent Countdowns. Written as 4 poems for each of the Sundays of Advent. Taking the topic celebrated when lighting the Advent candle but trying to make it as areligious as possible. In a world that was looking progressively darker being reminded of Hope, Faith, Joy and Peace felt like a good thing. This turned out to be an excellent addition to the countdown and increased weekly readership with a large spike every Sunday. Each year there is now an Advent Countdown to run alongside the Christmas Countdown.

December 1ˢᵗ — *Hope*

In this time of darkness,
Where the world seems bleak,
We are given one message,
Sunday this week,
As we light our candle,
With purple hue,
We are told to feel,
The hope in me and you.

December 8th — Faith

We light this candle for faith,
He holds a light to it in times of need,
And shine a light on it in times of hardship,
We ask for guidance from it in times of confusion.
***
Faith does not just mean religion,
You can have faith in many other things,
Such as the deep faith in love for one's family,
And the unmovable unbreakable faith in humanity.
***
Share your faith no mater its bases,
Show others where you get your strength,
Help others struggling to start finding theirs,
Let others known and learn from your strengths.

December 15th — Joy

It's the season of Joy,
Throughout the world,
Today we light,
The pink candle,
Think about joy,
The shepherd of mankind.
***

But while there is joy,
Spend a thought,
For the less unfortunate,
Who may not be joyous,
And may be under,
A dark cloud.
***

Outstretch your hand,
And gift some joy,
If you can make,
Just one person smile,
You can claim success,
Today and always.

December 22nd — Peace

At this time of darkness,
Where the nights feel never ending,
And the world feels broken,
We can often forget our humanity.
***
We try and push the dark,
Into a space in the back of our minds,
And keep thoughts of wars,
Suffering and pain for the new year.
***
So we light the last candle,
And bring to our mind's forefront,
The thoughts of peace,
And what part we play in the world.

New Year Countdown 2019

Another change in 2019 compared to 2018 was a complete New Year Countdown. At least one poem a day between the 25th December and the 1st January... You may also notice a 2nd of January. This is a nod to my homeland. In Scotland we get the 2nd of January off as a public holiday. The joke goes that, we party so hard for the New Year that we need a whole two days to recover.

December 25th — *Onward to New Year*

Now that the Turkey is done,
And the rum is run,
And Christmas draws to a close.
***
Thoughts turn to the year,
That the close is so near,
And the journey that is to come.
***
The end of a decade,
The start of a new one,
The possibilities that are to come.
***
So have another glass,
And toast to the past,
And watch the rest of the year pass.

December 26th — Boxing Day Rush

Quick grab your coat,
We don't want to miss the deals,
We need to get to town,
And spend money on those "Steals".
***

The kids have Christmas money,
Dad wants a new TV,
Mum wants a quiet life,
So let's go hit the high street.
***

Wrap up warm and snug,
Don't catch a winter bug,
Make your list and check it twice,
You want to buy something nice.

December 27th — Turkey Curry

With a twist of creativity,
Turkey can become a curry
Whether a masala or vindaloo,
There is a curry there for you.
***

Strips of Christmas turkey,
With a curry sauce of choice,
Some rice on the side,
And a pudding for the night.

December 28th — Sick of Turkey

Not again,
I hear you cry,
We had it yesterday,
You all sigh.
Never again,
You all will parade.
Not on my plate,
Will turkey be again.

December 29th — Boring Point in The Middle

In the boring mid-point,
Between Christmas and new year,
There is little on TV,
And no more cold beer.
***
Nothing exciting happens,
Within these short few days,
Offices are sat closed,
And have all played.

December 30th — Writing Resolution

Grab your pen and thinking cap,
Sit down and look for improvement,
And write this year's resolutions,
Just so we can all break them in January.
***

Or take the thing one step further,
And don't write resolutions at all,
Just aim for daily improvement,
And work to improve the world for all.

December 31st — Hello to A New Decade

Have a drink for today,
Shed a memory for yesterday,
Hold a thought for tomorrow.
***

Don't worry about today
Or dwell on the past,
And don't panic about the future.
***

We say goodbye to 2019,
Hello to a new decade,
And welcome to 2020.

January 1ˢᵗ — Happy New Year

Happy new year one and all,
It's a new decade,
And you can make it what you want.
***
There drink still in the fridge,
Puddings on the table,
You've had your fill of last year.
***
Welcome to the 20s of today,
And compare them to the past,
Will they be roaring as before.
***
Let us hope for the future,
And dream of this decade,
Let's make it what we can.

January 2nd — To The Scots

Happy New Year,
To my Scottish friends,
Who are just waking up,
From the New Year Bend,
***
We celebrate hard,
And sing our auld lang synes,
Shake hands with our families,
And welcome the time.
***
So with work tomorrow,
And a new year ahead,
It's probably time,
We start hitting the bed.

Christmas Countdown 2020

What a year 2020 turned out to be. It is unlikely anyone could have predicted all the events that occurred. Global pandemic and political mismanagement across the world leading to a once in a generation world shift. My life also switched gear. From a 9 to 5, Monday to Friday, office worker, to a working-from-home hermit that went out once a week. Not that I'm complaining, I've been the most productive I ever could have with the working from home change... Regardless of the constant cries of how "working form home is killing productivity" in the news.

2020 also saw the loss of a close member of my family. Once the strongest male influence on my life, my grandfather taught me a lot of my life skills. A true gentleman and a big supporter of my work. He left a huge hole in my life that will never be filled. As with a lot of people, death in a family brings out family politics that may have been unknown, and with that my family fractured... But I'll save that story for some kind of autobiography.

Lastly of note for 2020 was my decision to go back to university. Ever the gluten for punishment I did all the paperwork to start a part-time. remote MSc... Did I at least reduce my work hours to balance work, life and learning? No, I decided full-time work, 15 hours a week learning and a on-the-side online business was worth doing all at once... And through all that, I didn't stop writing poetry.

December 1ˢᵗ — Let It Begin

It's that time of year again,
Where I attempt to spread,
A little Christmas Cheer.
***

Another countdown,
To celebrate the season,
For another year.
***

24 sleeps to go,
Until Kris Kringle,
Will do his show.
***

So come join me,
For a month of poetry,
And let's make Christmas jolly.

December 2nd — Year in the Rearview

This year has been one no other,
A world shown to be humble,
In the face of something so small.
***

It was the year with the American Election,
And we all saw how that was run,
But what does it mean for the future.
***

A year where life was turned upside down,
And proved working from home could be done,
Without the need to see everyone.
***

The year where Samsung finally prevailed,
Releasing a screen that could fold,
Shaking off the image of the last one.
***

And more personally to me,
The year I published several works,
Proving my place in poetry.

December 3rd — Decorate the Tree

If you haven't done so already,
What are you waiting for,
Grab the Christmas tree,
Out of the loft,
Or pop to the shop,
And grab a new one.
***

It's time to build the cheer,
To create some excitement,
And get people to smile,
From ear to ear.
***

Nothing is more iconic,
At this time of year,
Than a big green tree,
Light up with LEDs,
Strings of tinsel,
And baubles here and there.

December 4th — Snowman

A man
Of snow,
Wrapped up cold,
A face,
Of ice spotted,
With coal,
A woollen scarf,
To keep,
Out the cold.
A body with a carrot,
For a colourful nose.
A game for kids,
To play in the snow.

December 5th — Christmas Crazes

The Coca-Cola trucks,
Won't be running this year,
So we need something,
To bring the Christmas cheer.
***
An inane and simple idea,
That sticks in everyone head,
That is recognised to all,
No matter when or where.

December 6th — Christmas is a Time for Family

Christmas is a time for family,
A time to look forward,
And look behind you.
***

A time to reflect,
On the years that have gone,
And those yet to come.
***

Take this time,
Make memories with it,
To think on them next year.

December 7th — Christmas Shopping

There is nothing I dread more,
Than going into town,
To buy the presents,
For my loved ones.
***

The busy cars,
With little parking,
The angry shoppers,
And the stress of hunting.
***

As I want to keep my town,
I will shop local to home,
Don't let the mammoths,
Of shopping win.
***

Just once a year,
The discomfort is,
In my humble opinion,
Worth it to keep the town.

December 8th — The Wrapping Waltz

First you cut the paper,
Then measure it twice,
Before you realise,
Somethings not write.
***

You try all positions,
To see if it will work,
Before you decide,
You need to restart.
***

You grab the paper roll,
Measure an extra touch,
Get ready to wrap,
And realise it's too much.
***

Once done with the paper,
It needs to be taped
One hand you hold the gift,
Trying not to let the paper escape.
***

The other hand tries to find,
The hidden little fine line,
On the roll of tape,
Before you resign.
***

You realise you need,
Both hands for the tape,
Two hands for the paper,

So it doesn't misshape.
***

The same every year,
The wrapping waltz,
One of the joys,
Of hiding what's in the box.

December 9th — Christmas Songs

Songs have the power to make it Christmas,
Whether it's the classics about the temperature outside,
Or proclamation about the wonderful time of the year,
Even a couple fighting about the Fairytale of New York.
***

Then there are the songs with no Christmas merit,
A list of a woman's favourite things like raindrops on roses,
Or that song covering desire and the power of love,
And we cannot forget the Let it snow! Let it snow! Let it snow!
***

Whatever is on your Christmas playlist,
There is definitely one thing we can all agree on,
Christmas isn't really Christmas until the music,
Has filled up every airway and taken control.

December 10th — Hanukkah

At this time of year,
It is easy to forget,
Other religions exist,
Other than Christianity.
***
Today marks the beginning,
Of the Jewish celebration,
Of the rededication,
Of the Second Temple in Jerusalem.
***
Hanukkah is a special time,
For a large number of people,
A time of remembrance,
And the lighting of the Menorah.
***
In this multi-cultural world,
It is worth learning other's beliefs,
And from that vein let me say,
Hanukkah Sameach! from me.

December 11th — Santa Visiting

The image of Santa rushing across the skies,
Lead by his nine favourites stars,
The flying four legged friends,
Pulling his sled from house to house.
***

We all know Dasher,
Named for his speed,
A race reindeer made to move,
Sprinting from tree to tree.
***

Then there's Dancer,
Majestic and elegant,
Just wanting to dance,
And let his moves shine.
***

Dancer's twin Prancer,
Is just as elegant,
And he knows it,
Keeping his antlers polished.
***

Vixen is next on the rope,
The distraction to the males,
She adds the touch of class,
To the riding group.
***

We then have Comet,
He's stubbornly loyal,
Named for the giant rock,

That landed when he was born.
***

Then there is cupid the romancer,
Born on Valentine's day,
He's a natural match maker,
But with no success for himself.
***

Donder also known as Donner,
She stands for thunder,
Married to Blitzen,
She is mother to the group.
***

Father Blitzen the brave,
Name stands for lighting,
Never known to back down,
He stands his ground.
***

Lastly there's Rudolph,
The baby of the group,
With his shiny red nose,
And his inexperienced hoofs.
***

When they ride as one,
You know that Santa has come,
His sled pulled by the best,
With majesty and the power.

December 11th — Acrostic Reindeer

Dasher the faster,
Always ahead,
Speed is his strength,
High in the sky,
Every reindeer,
Rides as one.
***

Dancer the star,
A stunning mover,
Never misses a,
Cha cha or waltz,
Even the day,
Right after Christmas.
***

Prancer, Dancer's twin brother,
Reindeer of majesty,
A sight of beauty,
Never a bad hair day,
Clearly blessed,
Excellently presented,
Rich in personality.
***

Vixen the most beautiful,
Immaculate looks,
Xena warier of the reindeer,
Elegant when flying,
Not a sign of stress.
***

Comet the loyal,
Of course named,
Mostly because of the rock,
Entering the atmosphere,
The exact time he was born.
***
Cupid the match-maker,
Unfortunately for him,
Picking his own match,
Is something that,
Doesn't come easy.
***
Donder the mother,
Of all the raider,
Name sometimes spelled,
Donner the thunder,
Each Christmas she,
Reigns her children in.
***
Blitzen the father,
Loves his wife he,
Is married to Donder,
Thunder and and Lightning,
Zappy together,
Enduring love,
No storm together.
***
Rudolph the red nose,
Unusual in his beacon,
Donder's last born,
Openly celebrated for,
Legendary heroics in 1939,

Pulling the sled in a storm,
He got every present delivered on time.

December 12th — Carollers

We hear the low drone,
And you know what is to come,
An out of tune and of beat rendition,
of a Christmas classic will be sung.
***
A 12 Days Of Christmas,
Or a Hark the Herold Angel Sing,
Whatever it is it always starts the same,
A low drone followed by the song.
***
You have to be a Grinch,
Not to enjoy hearing the bunch,
A group of people enjoying the chance,
To get out on the street and sing.
***
But when it finishes,
And you heart has been warmed,
After you have finished being wowed,
You are just glad it's done.

December 13th — Day of #NoH8

Christmas is a time for joy,
A time for friends and family,
And good will to all of mankind.
In the spirit of the season,
Continue as we want to go on,
And spread love rather than hate.
Together we can make good,
Make the world a better place,
By spreading joy and love not hate.
Since 2009 December the 13th,
Has been considered the day to,
Reflect on the world as the day of NoH8.

December 14th — Monkey Day

I must admit,
This has become,
An odd tradition,
For me to write,
A poem about,
Monkey Day.
***
But every year,
On this day,
I have written,
A small little,
Ditty about,
The Monkey.
***
Happy Monkey Day,
Whatever that means,
I hope you celebrate,
In whatever way,
You think is appropriate,
For this kind of day.

December 15th — When You Miss Someone

Christmas time can be hard,
When you remember those,
No longer around.
***
Family and friends that have left us,
To spend eternity,
Among the space dust.
***
The knowledge you can't say,
Merry Christmas to them,
Or wish them a happy new year.
***
When you miss someone,
It can play on your mind,
Even when you are having fun.
***
I like to imagine them with me,
Watching over me in life,
Sitting with me right here.

December 16th — Bauble

The elegance of a bauble,
It comes in all shapes and sizes,
All patterns and colours,
From the simple round,
To any shape imaginable,
The bauble dresses any tree,
And makes the fir more magical.
***
The,
Tree,
Bauble has,
A long history,
Of decorating trees,
Of hanging from branches,
And brightening up leaves,
A simple glass ball,
Symbolises a lot,
At this time,
Of year.

December 17th — Christmas At Home

It is become apparent,
This year will not be the same,
A large number of us,
Will not be getting together,
For that special day.
***
Let's hope that next year,
We can all meet in cheer,
And we can celebrate,
The way we want,
With those we hold dear.
***
For this year we will have to,
We celebrate Christmas at home,
And dream of better times,
That we know will come,
When all is said and done.

December 18th — Christmas Animals

Christmas cheer is spread each year,
With symbolism of things far and near.
One of the things that spreads the cheer,
Are the animals we link to this time of year.
But alongside the expected like reindeer,
Or the UK favourite the red breast robin,
There are some other animals known to show,
The symbolism we've learned to know.
Like the little donkey we all sing about,
Who carried Mary on her long old route.
Or the small straw yule tide goat,
Of the Scandinavian countries and now you know.
How about those hopping kangaroos,
Who lead Santa when he's down under.
Or the litany of birds we all recite in song,
When we sing about 12 days of Christmas long.
Each of these animals have their part to play,
In the Christmas magic on the build up to the day.

December 19th — Streets of White

No matter how often I see it,
I think, what a sight.
It can fall all day,
Or blanket the roads at night.
To this day I'm in aww,
When the roads turn white.
It masks the ground in cover,
Filling kids with delight.
And every so often,
Any changes it will overwrite.
There is not words deep enough,
To describe the feelings it can elicit.
To walk out of your door,
And see a change so explicit.

December 20th — Christmas Cards

The mantel has filled,
With cards from friends,
From far sides of the world,
And from family,
Who just live down the road.
***
Each card filled with well wishes,
Of a Happy or Merry Christmas,
And a hope for the New Year,
To be better than,
The ones we've left in the past.
***
Each card carries some love,
That fills up the spaces,
Above the fireplace,
Or on the hearth,
And in our hearts.

December 21st — Winter Solstice

But for those down in the south,
There's a day of light no night about,
Just the longest day to shout about.
***

And for those equatorial people,
There's no change in the day cycle,
Days and nights in one big circle.

December 22nd — Holly and Mistletoe

At Christmas Time,
We sing of mistletoe and wine,
Holly hanging in reefs,
And wood burning on the fires.
It's the time to rejoice,
The time we use our voice,
To spread cheer and love,
And are thankful for what we have.
A time to toast to life,
And acknowledge past strife,
To raise a glass to those,
Who are no longer with us.

December 23rd — Christmas Eve Eve

For most today is a working day,
Unless it falls on a weekend,
The eve to Christmas Eve,
The final build-up in excitement,
To those kids among us.
Each household has their own,
Traditions for the day,
Some Christmas movies,
Or board games in the eve,
How does your Christmas start.
It could be a sip of whisky,
Or a large sit down meal,
Some will listen to music,
Others will watch movies.
And some will ignore the day.
However your celebrations start,
It is now safe to say,
Christmas is well on its way,
Let the excitement grow,
And share it with those you know.

December 24th — Happy Birthday Dad

It still doesn't feel real,
Like a wound that won't heal.
You were always there,
And now will never be here.
I have felt pain, hate and anger,
But none of that will let me see you.
Unlike everyone else,
A birthday will no longer age you.
I can say happy birthday,
But you will not celebrate.
All I can live with are my thoughts,
And the lessons you have taught.

December 25th — Merry Christmas

Merry Christmas everyone,
The day is here,
Let's have some fun.
***
Celebrate with you kin,
Spread the joy,
With family and friends.
***
May your Christmas dreams,
Come true this year,
Let the countdown to New Year begin.
***
So toast with your drink,
To the Christmas day,
And watch the dinner shrink.

Advent Countdown 2020

The 2019 Advent Countdown was very well received and so 2020 had to have another. Just like 2019 it contained 4 poems celebrating Hope, Peace, Joy, and Love without making it religious. I believe that these four concepts are very important, regardless of which religion you follow, or none. And having 4 Sundays in a year to focus on them and help highlight them seems like something that should be done... Again... Regardless of your religious affiliations.

November 29th — Hope

Throughout this time we hope,
We think of lighter days,
When the world will be back,
And this will be in the past.
***

On this first Sunday of advent,
We light the candle of hope,
And invite the warmth within us,
For the future will be brighter.

December 6th — Peace

Peace is often just a concept,
Some distant idea in the mind,
No real representation in the world,
And a word that world leaders seem to dread.
***
But this year has shown us,
That Peace can be more real,
The world took a moment to breath,
And in that moment everything stood still.
***
The year started with promise,
And quickly turned to darkness,
In that darkness was a bright spark,
Showing us the feeling of unbridled peace.
***
The world has dark spots,
And life always has tough times
But in the darkest times think to peace,
That is one thing we can always aim towards.

December 13th — Joy

Joy to the world,
As so the song goes,
We celebrate a birth,
That was once foretold.
***

Peace on earth,
Was his life's aim,
To bring us all together,
In his living name.
***

Hark the herald,
Rejoice he's come,
To bring joy to earth,
And love to everyone.

December 20th — Love

Love comes in many forms,
From the love of a friend,
To the love of a relative,
The love of a partner,
To the love of a stranger.
***

In this time of reflection,
Reflect on those you love,
Those who bring joy,
The ones no longer with us,
And the ones we've left behind.
***

Turn your thoughts form pain,
In the spirit of love today,
Send love out to the world,
In everything you say,
Share love in your way.

New Year Countdown 2020

On the run down to the end of the first year of the 2020's there was yet another full New Year Countdown. This featured some poetry that appeared to have become traditional. From the poem lamenting another turkey based meal to a poem celebrating the 2nd of January, writing 2020 felt like the new year countdown had always been part of the mix. But in that mix was the bitter sting of knowing life could never go back to the way it was in 2019.

December 26th — Boxing Day

Boxing Day this year will be unusual,
No rush on the shops,
No queues for the deals,
Just a quiet day in,
With the ones we love.
***
But for those on their own,
Spare a thought today,
Give them a call,
Let them know you are there,
Show them you care.
***
Let's create a new boxing day tradition,
Rather than out shopping,
Let's stay home and veg,
why not close the shops instead,
And give a rest to those working.

December 27th — Turkey Again

During the year,
We romanticise turkey,
Then comes the Christmas,
And we love it with trimmings,
But everyone forgets,
The days that follow,
Where people get creative,
With the left over meat thinnings.
***
Some try a curry,
Others try sandwiches,
There are those more creative,
That may be more adventurous,
But every year it is the same,
We finish Christmas dinner,
And don't want to look,
At a turkey again!

December 28th — Limbo

There is an awkward few days,
Between Christmas and New Year,
Where time makes no sense,
And passage seems to freeze.
A strange kind of limbo,
That breaks the TV schedule,
And leave us all confused,
Asking when's the evening news.

December 29th — *Resolutions*

It's that time of year,
Where we resolve,
To write resolutions,
We plan to stick to resolutely.
***
We set our goals,
For us to achieve,
In the twelve months,
Until the next year.
***
Some people resolve,
To spend time with family,
Do something they find scary,
Or just practice something they love.
***
While others resolve,
To ditch those bad habits,
To get back in shape,
Or just to break a downward spiral.
***
Whatever you resolve,
You can achieve it,
Believe in yourself,
And you will see it through.

December 30th — Year In Review

We now creep to the end,
Of the strange year we are in.
***

Looking back is always useful,
So here is 2020 in review.
***

There is a lot for me,
To be grateful for this year,
But first let's get the bad out of the way.
***

This year I lost my grandfather,
A man of many talents of much laughter,
A strong pillar of my life,
No longer hear tonight.
***

I caught the virus,
Just last month,
And it floored me,
Something I still suffer.
***

My wedding was postponed,
Not cancelled,
And will still go-ahead next year.
***

Now that the bad is acknowledged,
Let's look to the good,
And celebrate where we can.
***

This year was musical,
With more time at the piano,
And taking up the violin.
***
There was also my book,
That hit the shelves this year,
And almost reached an Amazon no. 1.
***
Working from home gave me freedom,
To make working as comfortable as possible,
And aided towards a promotion.
***
All of these things I am grateful for,
And these are just the shortlist,
Next year will be better,
I am certain of this.
***
Last of all to review is you,
But that is a topic for its own poem,
Don't you think?

December 31st — You

As we close out 2020,
And open up 2021,
I'm still humbled each day,
By your continued support.
***
In 2020 you supported me,
When I released a new book,
Your support has helped me,
Keep this page online.
***
Without you there would be no me,
And by extension no Pesky Poetry®,
There would be no Christmas Countdown,
Or random fruit poems.
***
Each piece of support,
From a like to a share,
Keeps my work alive,
And shows you care.
***
So let me exclaim,
From the bottom of my heart,
Thank you for your support,
Thank you for your likes,
Thank you for your shares,
Thank you for your time,
But most importantly,
Thank you for you!

January 1st — Happy New Year

Happy New Year,
From me to you,
Let's hope this one,
Bring love to you,
Let it bring joy,
And happiness too,
As we move on,
From the last year,
To something new.

January 2ⁿᵈ — The Second

For those not aware,
Today is a holiday,
For the Scottish out there.
***

We nurse the hangover,
From Hogmanay,
Right through to today.
***

So Happy New Year,
To my Scottish friends,
I hope the hangover ends.

Christmas Countdown 2021

2021 was a long year, a few life events were supposed to happen that didn't and a few that weren't supposed to did. But still, I sat down and wrote the Christmas Countdown for it's 10th year... Ok, 9th if you include the gap. By this point the Christmas Countdown was a given and I think this was the first year I really noticed what had been achieved.

December 1st — Let the Countdown Commence

It's that time of year again,
Advent's begun,
November has come to an end.
***
We start the countdown,
To Christmas,
And the new year beyond.
***
We reminisce on the year,
Buy presents,
Plan for tomorrow.
***
Let the season begin,
To spread love,
And joy to all men.

December 2nd — Memories of Christmas

There are three schools of people,
The kind who chip in with:
"It doesn't feel like winter,
because the ground is still green."
Or those who exclaim:
"It doesn't feel like winter,
It's getting colder each year."
And lastly those who don't comment at all.
***

For each year is different to the last,
And we can never have them back.
We live with the footage and pictures,
But most importantly the memories.
In the patchwork quilt of life,
There are big bright square for Christmas night.

December 3rd — Decorate the Tree

Blow the dust off the top,
Time to get the tree out of the loft.
***
Now find the trinkets,
All the bits and bobbles,
And the fairy or star for the top.
***
Uncoil the tinsel,
Place it on the tree,
Haphazard of very planned.
***
Untangle the lights,
Give them a quick test,
And make sure they are all right.
***
Find that one,
The random decoration,
You built at school many a moon ago.
***
Take a step back,
Marvel at the decoration,
Start counting down until it goes back.

December 4th — Christmas Lights

Twinkle Twinkle little light,
Making each evening bright,
Spreading Christmas cheer,
At this time of year,
Twinkle Twinkle Christmas light,
Brightening up someone's night.

December 5th — *Footsteps in the Snow*

My eyes look down,
As I miss you this year,
It's been so long,
Since you were here.
***
The sound of your voice,
The gifts that you gave,
Are all memories now,
Of Christmas far away.
***
My eyes drift down,
And see footprints there,
Walking next to me,
Where you once were.
***
A tear comes to my eye,
And I wish you were here,
To comfort me when I'm sad,
In the dark of the year.
***
My eyes clear up,
And I see the footprints clear,
You were always beside me,
You are always there.

December 6th — Christmas Cards

Have you got your list?
Have you checked it twice?
Counted the stamps you need tonight?
Christmas cards need sending out.
***
Checked the addresses?
Removed those you don't know?
Written the envelopes?
Is it time that they go?
Christmas cards are going tonight.

December 7th — Holly and Wine

Hang the Holly on your door,
Heat the mulled wine on the stove,
Crack the board games out,
And play the classics on the radio.
***

Get the gingerbread men,
If that's your thing,
And decorate them,
With sugar and icing.
***

End the night with a movie,
A Christmas ghost or three,
Something with a Christmas spirit,
Maybe Scrooge, but with muppets.

December 8th — Hot Toddy

On these cold winter nights,
The throat takes a bite,
The air nips the voice,
And you feel rather horse.
***
A quick dash of whiskey,
Some honey or syrup,
Add a splash of lemon,
Some hot water,
And you will be singing.
***
Nothing quite sooths,
Like the sharp ness of you,
A sip of your warm spirit,
And it lifts my spirits.

December 9th — Snow On The Ground

The ground is blanketed white,
By a secret visitor,
Silent in the night.
***
Like something out of a movie,
The ground is pure,
The world unmoving.
***
A blank canvas is revealed,
Where once was,
The ground levelled.
***
The tools for building in snow,
Creating snow families,
Or igloo to show.
***
This is all very temporary,
It will melt,
And could be gone tomorrow.

December 10th — *Robin Red Breast*

Robin red breast,
Looking so fine,
Hopping around all the time.
***
Leaving shapes,
In the snow,
So you know where he goes.
***
With his brown,
And white feathers,
And red chest so bright.
***
You are iconic,
On a cold winter's night.

December 11th — Love And Good Will To All People

May your nights be merry,
May your days be bright,
May you get all you wish for,
Come day or night.
***
Know that your loved,
Know that your beautiful,
Know that you have friends,
And that's undisputable.
***
Live in the now,
Live for today,
Live for your friends,
And you family.
***
Be true to yourself,
Be who you are,
Be who you want,
No matter how bizarre.
***
Share your love,
Share your sunshine,
Share your good will,
To all people.

December 12th — The Sproutlight

Once a year,
It gets a cheer,
And by some a jeer.
***
The humble sprout,
Is what it's about,
At this time of year.
***
Plates abound,
With the green,
Little ball round.
***
For some,
A Christmas treat,
That's neat to eat.
***
For others,
A troubled veg,
On the Christmas table.
***
It's time,
Has come to bathe,
In it's limelight
***
Wherever you stand,
On the humble bud,
You can't steal it's sproutlight.

December 13th — Dalliance With Decadence

Let the frills abound,
Drink only the best around,
In this time of frivolity,
A dalliance with decadence.
***

Only the very best,
At this time of year,
Spare not the rest,
In this sardoodledom of celebration.

December 14th — Christmas Luau

Do you ever just want to get away,
To somewhere warm and sandy,
At this dark time of year,
Wouldn't it be satisfy,
To sit on a beach with a beer?
***
Maybe a burger on the BBQ,
Or a hotdog from a stand,
The wave lapping up,
Against the golden sand,
Isn't it nice to dream?
***
Somewhere warm as a retreat,
Sunny and somewhere sweet,
Have a Christmas party,
Of a different kind,
A luau for Christmas time.

December 15th — 10 Days To Go

Were in the final run,
The ten day countdown,
The presents are bought,
The wrapping is done,
All that's left is excitement,
And the day of fun.
***
So sit back and enjoy,
As Christmas takes hold,
Watch all the movies,
And TV series of old,
Reminisce of past Christmases,
And stay warm from the cold.

December 16th — *Snowman*

Those black beady eyes,
Keep watch from my back yard.
A smile dark as coal,
Makes the snow less cold.
With a woollen scarf,
To keep the chill off it's back.
A carrot for a nose,
With hiding what it knows.
Frozen in place,
As if held by deep fright.
Will it still be there,
After the long cold night?

December 17th — Schools Out

Schools out for winter,
The kids get a break,
The parents get a headache.
***
Time for snowball fights,
Skidding on the ice,
And sledding down the hill.
***
No need for early mornings,
Or school uniforms,
Just spending time with dads and mums.

December 18th — Visiting Family

Spread Christmas cheer,
by visiting family this year.
Do the Santa run,
Share laughter and fun.
Bring a smile and joy,
To each girl and boy.
Hug those you haven't seen,
Since before Halloween.
Visit those you see once a year,
And let them know you hold them dear.

December 19th — Yule Log

One of the many treats,
Of the end of the year,
Is the chocolate log,
Some of us hold dear.
***
A chocolate sponge,
Draped in chocolate icing,
With chocolate cream,
Is just divine.
***
As an after dinner dessert,
Or just a sweet snack,
A tiny sliver,
Or half of a pack.
***
Nothing beats a piece,
Of the chocolate treat,
With a cup of tea,
On a cold Christmas evening.

December 20th — Dreaming of What's Under the Tree

Every child's dreams,
Should now be consumed,
By guesses,
Of what's under the tree.
***
A new bike for mike,
A doll for little mols,
Something,
For the older bro.
***
As for mum and dad,
They are excited to see,
The looks,
On their little faces.

December 21st — Winter Solstice

The Christians have Christmas,
The Pagans, Yuletide,
And the Romans,
Have Saturnalia,
Whatever its name,
The idea is the same,
To celebrate the darkness away.
***
Nights of debauchery,
Or saintly singing,
For some it's the logs,
They will be burning,
Whatever your ritual,
The idea stays the same,
We all get together and spread love to all men.
***
When the sun sets tonight,
We know it will rise again,
And the days will get brighter,
Again and again,
Whatever the day,
The idea stays the same,
Tomorrow will come, again and again.

December 22nd — Christmas TV Schedule

What day is it?
Followed by rustling,
Is a sure sign the holidays,
Are now in full swing.
***

For some it's tradition,
For others it's their mission,
To watch the holiday specials,
From the TV guide.
***

It's the seasonal movie,
Which isn't about Christmas,
It's the soaps that must make a scene,
To keep its viewers.
***

Whatever you poison,
Grab that tv guide,
And check what's on,
It'll be Christmas soon.

December 23rd — Stockings Up

Not long now,
'till the jolly man comes,
With his cheeks of red,
And is sacks of fun.
***
Now clear a spot,
On the mantle place,
To put you stocking,
For Santa is coming.
***
For the jolly red man,
Is on his way,
And he needs somewhere to put,
The toys he made.
***
Hang you stocking,
With care up over there,
And wait with restrain,
To see what it contains.

December 24th — One Sleep To Go

Tonight's the night,
When the big man will come,
With his reindeer in tow,
And the sack upon his back.
***
Landing on the roof,
With one job to do,
Bring a smile to your face,
If you have been good.
***
Get to bed early,
And don't stir when you hear,
Old St Nic on the roof,
With gifts to spare.

December 25th — Merry Christmas

A decade of Christmas Countdowns,
Comes to an end today,
Poems of all sorts,
From Santa's beard to sleigh.
But the 25th is always reserved,
For me to say.
Merry Christmas to you and your family,
To your friends and your pets.
May you get the gifts you want,
And happiness that never ends.

Advent Countdown 2021

Although it is one of the shortest countdowns, containing only 4 poems, the Advent Countdown is one of my most popular. At this point I'm not sure if it's the messaging or the fact that it's linked to a religious event. Whatever it is, I enjoy writing these four poem. The set structure of Hope, Peace, Joy & Love gives a perfect warmup to get the creativity flowing.

Advent in 2021 was written when I was in a dark place myself. Having lost close relatives in previous years and struggling to come to terms with a family rift, it was proving hard to keep hope, peace, joy and love alive. So I turned to writing, taking on some big projects and wiring several MSc papers... And, the Advent Countdown gave me time to reflect on these things and sort out my thoughts.

November 27th — *Hope*

In our darkest hour,
The last thing left,
Is our supply of hope.
***
Hold on to that tightly,
And never let it go.
***
No matter how deep,
The hole around you is,
Keep the glimmer of hope.
***
From that small spark,
A lot of good can come.
***
Repeat after me,
I am worthy of hope,
And my hopes are valid.

December 4th — Peace

People take peace for granted,
As a fundamental part of life.
But not everyone is so lucky,
And peace is hard fought for.
***
In an ever fractured world,
Peace looks harder to keep.
More and more we fight,
And those fights risk the peace.
***
From war-torn countries,
To the family disputes.
peace shouldn't just be known,
It should be lived and understood.
***
Repeat after me,
I deserve peace,
Peace is my right,
And no-one can say otherwise.

December 11th — Joy

Joy to the world,
We are alive for another day,
The world keeps spinning,
Let the small things melt away.
***
Feel joy to be,
And keep joy in you today,
Take in a deep breath,
And breath the negative away.
***
Smile wide,
Let that smile spread,
Make it contagious,
And bring joy to another's day.
***
Repeated after me,
I am joy incarnate,
I have the joy in me,
And nobody can take it away.

December 18th — Love

Love to your kin,
And to you too,
Know that you are loved in all you do.
***
You must love you,
Like everyone does,
Love yourself in all that you do.
***
Everyone needs love,
You are no different,
Love everyone in all that they do.
***
Repeat after me,
I deserve love,
I deserve to be loved,
And no-one can say otherwise.

New Year Countdown 2021

The end of 2021 saw most places in the UK back to a sense of "normal" post covid... This meant that postponed life events could finally be planned and life could continue after the short break. The New Year Countdown contained the usual topics; that weird downtime between Christmas and New Year, having turkey for the umpteenth time, but it was lacking a January 2nd Poem for the Scottish.

December 25th — *Final Countdown*

As Christmas comes to a close,
We turn our attention,
To the year on the approach.
***

2021 has been unique,
We can all agree,
And we all pray for something less bleak.
***

Take a moment to look back,
Think of only the good,
Leave the dark behind.
***

2022 is another world,
A clean slate to work with,
On this never ending earth.

December 26th — *First Toy Casualty*

Parents know it too well,
The hours after the day,
A child will cry,
And a toy thrown away.
***
There is always one toy,
That doesn't see new year,
That a kid will break,
And claim it was just sitting there.
***
Some will try and fix it,
Others will just be replaced,
And for some,
The toy will be thrown in the waste.
***
So spare a thought for those toys,
Lost, broken or destroyed,
And let that question built,
Which toy will next be killed.

December 27th — Sick of Turkey

What will it be,
Curry or soup,
With veg,
Boiled or steamed?
***

This conundrum plays out,
In households all around,
Not to waste turkey,
When so much is around.
***

For lunch it's a sandwich,
Or just cold slice,
Or with some sauce,
Whatever is nice.
***

But by today,
Most can say,
There just getting,
Sick of turkey.

December 28th — The In-between Time

We're at that awkward time,
When time's lost all meaning,
Looking at the TV Schedule,
Is the only way it's keeping.
***

That dark strange lull,
At the end of the year,
Where days come together,
Into one long blur.
***

It must end soon,
Of that you know,
But exactly when,
We don't though.

December 29th — Too Soon

Would it be taboo,
Or considered too soon,
If I was thinking about Christmas 2022?
***
Given the bad year,
I've needed some cheer,
And what better way than thinking,
Of Christmas next year?
***
By then we will meet,
Without masks on our cheeks,
We will be able to sing along,
To Christmas Carols and Songs.
***
Let us forget this year,
And look forward to the next,
Which will be more like they were in the past.

December 30th — New Year's Resolutions

Years ago I resolved,
To resolution no more,
And this year is no different.
No arbitrary set goal,
Or hating myself for failing,
I resolve to not resolute.
Rather I will stretch,
Aim for constant improvement,
Without setting random goals.
The conundrum is,
Resolving not to resolution,
Was a New Year's resolution of its own.

December 31st — Goodbye 2021

Goodbye 2021,
Good riddance to you,
You won't be remembered,
For being filled with love and joy.
***
2020 had such hope,
2021 Was meant to save that,
And now that's all up to you 2022,
Please, oh please, don't let us down.
***
But before,
We lock the door,
On the book of 2021,
Let's take a look back once.
***
Find one thing,
That truly made you happy,
Hold it in the front of your mind,
Keep that as your memory of 2021.
***
Remember the people,
Everyone all around you,
Those people who were there,
To suffer, side-by-side, 2021 with you.
***
Of course there were dark times,
Of course there were bleak days,
But focus on the good around,

And try to forget the negative.

January 1st — Happy New Year

And so we have made it,
Another year is gone,
A new one is here.
***

Happy New Year,
2022 is full of promise,
Let's see what comes.
***

May your 2022,
Be better than 2021,
And be the best it can.
***

May my muses,
Continue to inspire,
My writing hand.
***

And may the world,
Become brighter,
Than in 2021.

Christmas Countdown 2022

2022 ended a very whirlwind year. Never doing wedding planning again. Got married! Completed a chunk of my MSc. Alongside all that I wrote poetry and managed to complete the Christmas Countdown all over again.

December 1ˢᵗ — It begins

The nights are getting longer,
The air is getting colder,
The holidays are getting closer,
That can only mean one thing,
Christmas is on its way.
***

And with Christmas comes this,
A countdown in poem form,
Day by day a verse shall there be,
Until the big day has come.
***

Join me on this adventure,
A poem to decorate the tree,
Something to mark the days,
Until we can all be together,
With friends and family.

December 2nd — Defrost the Singers

They've been awoken,
Stretched off the year,
Exercised their voices,
For the Christmas season.
***
Get the Bublé on,
And have yourself,
A Merry Little Christmas,
Or just sing Santa Baby.
***
Hark! The Herald Carey Sings,
Of a Silent Night,
Or O Holy Night,
And Santa Claus is Comin' to Town.
***
They will sing,
For the next month,
Before they go back,
Into hibernation again.

December 3rd — First Snow Fall

It all begun one cold dark night,
The sky was white,
The streetlights bright,
The wind was a sigh,
And carried a nip,
Before down fell,
The little white bit.
***
Piece by piece,
The sky fell down,
 Littering the area,
Where once there was ground,
Hiding the dark,
With a layer of wite,
All within one dark night.
***
A white canvas it leaves,
Full of endless,
Unimaginable Possibilities,
For everyone and everything,
The first crunch,
Under a foot,
To the final melt.

December 4th — Holidays are Coming

The holidays are coming,
You can see it all around,
from the change in leaves,
to the change in shelves,
To the lights going up around.
***
Soon the stores will battle,
For the best yuletime ad,
And all the deals will come out,
aimed at mums and dads,
For their darling or their brat.
***
Soon lists will be written,
Of toys that everyone wants,
The latest kids' fad,
Or the latest thing to have,
All neatly tied in a box.

December 5th — There's A Robin On My Shoulder

There's a robin by my shoulder,
He hums his little song,
Of the Christmas to come,
and the Christmases gone,
He whistles of snowball fights,
And sledding down the hills.
***
He's seen them all over the years,
The Christmases come and gone,
Listened to laughter and cheers,
From children now moved on,
Seen the fairytale love stories,
From couples with life to share.
***
He's now off on his rounds again,
To spread the Christmas cheer,
Another Christmas ahead of him,
Not sure what it will bring,
The robin and his magic touch,
Will certainly be there.

December 6th — *Postman With Cards*

I see him,
With his big red sack,
No it's not Santa,
The postie is back,
With his bag of mystery.
***
What surprises,
Are in there for me?
A card from a friend,
A parcel for me,
Or something else entirely.
***
Thank you postie,
For your part,
At this time of year,
For bringing cards,
And Joy to me.

December 7th — Christmas Pets

I am for life,
Not just for Christmas.
***

Not just a toy,
To pack away,
When you're done with.
***

I need attention,
Every day of the week,
Not just when you feel you need me.
***

If you cant commit,
Then please leave me be.
***

Another home,
Will find me,
With the right family.
***

So think twice when buying a pet,
They are not a Christmas Present,
The are a long term bet.

December 8th — Christmas Jumper Day

Let's all dress up warm,
Dress up all jolly,
Get the holiday spirit on,
Spread the joy,
In the new old fashioned way!
***
Whether it lights up,
Or has snow,
Share your joy,
With every man woman,
Girl and boy.
***
Let's all dawn,
Our Christmas Jumpers,
And wear them everywhere,
Spread a smile,
On every face.

December 9th — Be Vewy Vewy Quiet I'm Hunting A Furr Twee

Whether it's a thick fir,
Or a spruce or pine,
It's that time of year,
We hunt them down.
***

You've got to sneak up,
No noise in the snow,
Don't want to spook it,
Before you go for the chop.
***

As it falls to the ground,
The work is half done,
You've got to cart it down,
Back to the front room.
***

On a silent night,
Of hunting trees,
You've got to be stealthy,
To get what you seek.

December 10th — Writing Christmas Cards

Write them for the family,
For the friends of old,
Pen one to that neighbour,
And one to that couple,
You know the one,
You met on holiday.
***
Write your well wishes,
To those you write,
Only at this time of year,
And spread your own brand,
Of Christmas Cheer.
***
But get them posted soon,
You don't want to miss,
The last red breast robin,
On his rounds of the year.

December 11th — Elf on the Shelf on Pesky Poetry

A craze that swept the world,
Putting a stuffed toy on a shelf,
And convicting young wards,
That the elf reports back to the big man.
***
But what if it's true,
And he is watching you,
Smugly from his shelf,
Judging you for himself.
***
Wherever you are,
Wherever it is,
Be on your best behaviour,
As he stays on his.

December 12th — *Mistletoe and Time*

It's Cliff Richard's Time,
Mistletoe and Wine,
Adults singing,
Out of tune,
Christmas Rhymes.
***

There's crumbs on the carpet,
And the kings on TV,
A time to be thankful,
In the things that we have.
***

It's Christmas Time,
Mistletoe and rhyme,
Were all singing,
Christmas tunes,
***

With love for our families,
And gifts to you and me,
Let's all be joyous,
For the singers we hear.

December 13th — Ask Santa

Have you written your list,
Have you checked it twice,
Found out which toy,
Is naughty or nice.
***

Have you sent your list,
With excuses galore,
To Santa Claus,
At the north pole.
***

Are you waiting patiently,
By the fireplace,
For the thud on the roof,
As the reindeers take their place.
***

Counting down the days,
Till the presents appear,
Next to the tree,
For another year.

December 14th — Stocking Filler

Take a giant sock,
Hung by the chimney with care,
In the hopes that a gift,
May be found in there.
***

Come Christmas morn,
When the daybreak's light,
Wakes the children,
From an exciting night.
***

Have fortunes been paid,
Or coal pieces in place,
For the child that should open,
After saying grace.

December 15th — 10 Ho Ho Ho

It's as iconic as one, two, three,
Or as recognisable as a, b, c,
Said with a smile,
And a laugh from the belly,
The sound of the big man,
Can make us all jolly,
When you hear the Ho Ho Ho,
You just have to know,
That Santa is on his way.

December 16ᵗʰ — I Saw Daddy Kissing Santa

I saw daddy kissing Santa Clauses,
He was underneath the mistletoe,
He said that mummy,
Shouldn't have all the fun,
Before Santa had to go.
***
With his rosy cheeks,
And a cheeky smile,
Santa kissed goodnight,
Before flying north,
On his sleigh,
Led by star light.
***
I saw Santa kissing Daddy,
Next to the Christmas tree,
After unloading his sack,
Of amazing gifts,
And presents for me.

December 17th — Saturnalia

While we have Christmas spirit,
The Romans had Saturnalia,
A raucous celebration,
Of gift giving and partying,
And fun for all men around,
Indeed a contemporary Catullus,
Once called it "The best of days."
***

Let's honour the Roman ways,
And celebrate with each other,
On the run up to Christmas day,
Get raucous and merry,
Sing loudly and dance badly,
But leave the human sacrifice,
In those bygone days.

December 18th — Snow Family

There's snow family,
Like this family,
Of all families,
Like us.
There's snow way,
To celebrate Charismas,
Like this way,
Like now.
There's snow Christmas,
Like this Christmas,
Like no Christmas,
With fuss.

December 19th — Good Will To All Men

Goodwill to all men,
Is more poignant this year,
As Christian sentiment,
It comes as a shock,
With what is going on in the world.
***
Take a moment,
Just this Christmas,
Spare a thought,
For those in Kyiv,
Who are under the barrage of war.
***
How can a country,
That claims to be Christian,
Act in this way,
Against another county,
Against goodwill to all men.
***
Take a second,
And give a prayer,
Keep in your mind,
All those out there,
And always give goodwill to all humans.

December 20*th* — *Past, Present and Yet To Come*

Cast your mind to Christmas Past,
Those years left behind,
The joy the love the laughs,
Of friends and family around,
How time has changed,
Since those days of old.
***

Now think of Christmas Present,
A time we make ourselves,
With friends of old and of new,
Giddy like garden elves,
Another year of new memories,
While we remember those of past.
***

Consider Christmas yet to come,
A blank canvas in the mind,
With years of possibilities,
All future Christmas undefined,
A plethora of exciting stories,
Just waiting there to be found.

December 21st — Sol Sistere

Twice a year,
The sun stands still,
In the sky,
As if God's will.
***

For those up north,
This brings cold,
For those south,
Summers of gold.
***

Sol Sistere,
The sun stands still,
Neither benevolent,
Or malevolent.
***

It observers us below,
With gentle light,
Pausing to peek,
On our lives.

December 22nd — What Makes A Good Tree

Is it the tinsel,
Or the baubles,
Or the glitter,
Or the angel?
Is it the hight,
Or the width,
The branches,
Or the base?
Is it the gifts,
Or the wrapping,
Or the placement,
Or the meaning?
What is it that,
Makes a tree special,
When it's in a house,
And covered in tinsel?

December 23rd — Christmas Eve Eve

It's an odd day,
Christmas Eve Eve,
Not quite the day before,
But Christmas somehow feels closer.
***

For some it's the break before the madness,
Some it's just the start of gladness,
For other's it's the wrapping day,
And there are others that,
Would rather not say.
***

However you spend you're day,
Let the sprit start flowing,
Humm a Christmas jingle,
And get ready for old Kris Kringle.

December 24th — Mary and Joseph Rode a Donkey

That perilous night,
2000 years ago,
A mother and father to be,
Went on the long road,
Or so the story goes.
***
Whether you follow,
Or you chose not to,
The story of hope,
Is one we can all share,
***
The hope of new birth,
A hope for the future,
The hope we all desire,
A hope to hold on to,
The hope we live with.
***
So shed a thought,
For the Mary and Joseph of today,
On their own long journey,
From home to away.

December 25th — Merry Christmas

Merry Christmas,
Is such a simple phrase,
That conveys great meaning,
To those who use it.
So let me take this time,
And wish you and yours well,
Merry Christmas my readers,
And wish the Christmas Countdown farewell!

December 25th — Christmas Present Massacre

They felt the ground moving,
From their hiding place under the tree.
The thudding of steps,
From the enemy.
Then all of a sudden,
With a shudder and a jolt.
They were in the grasp,
Of the enemies claws.
Unceremoniously moved,
To be alone.
Before being unwrapped,
With the contents on show.
The great cleanup,
Now begins.
Where all the wrapping paper,
Gets rammed in the bins.
Thus signalling the end,
Of the Christmas Tree massacre.

Advent Countdown 2022

Hope, Peace, Joy and Love, the real four elements of life. At this point the Advent Countdown is almost twice as popular as the Christmas Countdown by total reader count. Not to mention that 2022 saw a tripling in readers from the year before. Pesky Poetry has one of the most amazing communities and would not be where it is without the love from the community. The poetry continues to bring me joy and knowing there are people out there who enjoy it brings me peace... And while I write this I have real hope for 2023.

November 27th — Hope

As we reach the end,
Of another year,
We sit around,
And spread the cheer,
Think of the good,
That's in the past,
With a glass full of hope,
For what is yet to pass.

December 4th — Peace

What does peace really sound like,
Is it the sound of waves on a beach,
Or the silence of a midnights sleep.
How does peace really look,
The white of a thousand lights,
Or the darkness of a unlit room.
Peace means many things,
To every different person.
Wishing you all the peace,
That you deserve,
From this day forward.

December 11th — Joy

There are many forms of joy,
At this time of year,
From a child's joy of Christmas,
To the joy of a nice beer,
The joy of a grand parent,
Seeing their grand child,
Or the joy of a snow bird,
Finding a seed pile.
***
Even in the darkest time,
Joy is all around us,
You don't need to look for it,
Just need to recognise it,
And let it find us.

December 18th — Love

Love thy neighbour as thyself,
The famous words in Matthew,
Attributed to Jesus of Nazareth.
Even those who don't practice,
Often agree with the sentiment,
To love everyone without resentment.
In this world of new wars,
We must all remember,
We are all humans, everyone together.
So love each other, as you do yourself.
And share that love with everyone else,
Remember we are all human, at the end of the day,
We are all struggling, in the same way.

New Year Countdown 2022

And here comes the end of the 2022 countdown. What a year it was. Celebrating the Platinum Jubilee and then the loss of Queen Elizabeth II, the ever increasing bleak images coming out of Ukraine, or breaking the 8 billion human mark... 2022 will go down like no other in my life. Queen Elizabeth II was presented with two poems in celebration of her Jubilee and I still have the beautiful letter returned by her Lady-in-waiting.

December 25th — New Year Begins

We now pass from this period,
Of Christmas Countdown cheer,
And move in to the lull,
Before the new year.
A time to reminisce,
On all that has happened,
And a time to sleep off,
All that's been eaten.
Take a moment just now,
To look all around you,
And appreciate those,
Who spent today with you.

December 26th — Second Christmas Dinner

There is stuffing,
And potatoes,
And maybe some sprouts,
All from yesterday,
Let's get it all out.
And who could forget,
The star of the show,
More turkey for dinner,
That must not be thrown.
So why not have a feast,
A second Christmas Dinner,
If you will with food and joy,
Let yesterday overflow.

December 27th — Turkey, Love or Hate It?

It's somewhat tradition,
In the New Year Countdown,
To lament the turkey,
And it's unending presence.
The whole year goes by,
And not a moan for the bird,
Then Christmas comes,
And it's as if nobody has heard.
The culinary specialists,
Will make curry and soups,
Maybe something more exotic,
With spices and roots.
After Christmas it must be,
The most hated meat on the table,
Yet all year round it's a meat staple,
Earning the title, the favourite most hated meat.

December 28th — Neither Now, Nor Later

We are in that not time,
Neither this year nor next,
Nether holiday nor working,
Some strange point,
Between the vale of years..
The gap where tv goes strange,
Daytime merges with night,
And all that sparkles,
Is no longer Christmas Lights.
But onwards we go,
Towards the next celebration,
A day of such promise,
Another clean slate,
A year to try again.

December 29th — Have the Chocolates Lasted

Have you beaten temptation,
Or has it gotten the better of you.
Have you saved any for later,
Or snaffled it in one sitting.
Will there be any for New Year,
Or just wrappers left behind.
Have you managed your hands,
Or could you not keep them off.
Are you saying "Just one more",
It's Christmas after all,
Or are you saving some for later,
Once you've eaten all from the family bowl.

December 30th — New Year's Resolutions

Writing New Year's resolutions,
Is not easy to do,
How do you chose,
What is most important to you,
That is why for this year,
I resolve just one thing,
To be better than the person,
I'm leaving behind.

December 31st — Tonight is the Night

Tonight's the night,
The year end is here,
This year draws to a close,
And a new year is near,
Where we drink,
And get merry,
And shed off this year,
We see in the new,
With a big cheer.
As this year draws to an end,
May the next year be happy,
May your dreams come true,
And may your days be full.

January 1ˢᵗ — Happy New Year

Midnight passes,
Country by country,
Seeing in a new day,
And bringing a new year.
For those countries I say,
Happy New Year,
Selamat tahun Baru,
Bonne année,
Feliz año nuevo,
◊◊◊◊,
And to all the other languages.

January 2nd — Happy New Year

What a year it has been,
Both personally and globally,
With such news,
As the death of the Queen,
Or the celebration,
Of her platinum jubilee,
And the self destruction,
Of the UK government.
Worldwide it's been huge,
With the war in Ukraine,
Where Bush slipped up,
In his own special way,
And the surpassing,
Of 8 billion human beings.
2022 will go down in history,
As a year like no other,
And yet it is now just that,
History!
Happy New Year,
From the Pesky Poet.

December 25th — A Scottish New Year

New Year Countdown 2022, January 2nd

Th' scots hae got,
iI a' figured out,
A day o' rest,
To git ower th' drink,
To git rid o' th' hangover,
Of th' nicht afore th' nicht before.
You see,
Us scots,
Celebrate sae hard,
We lose a day outright.
So tak' a leaf,
From th' book we wrote,
Party sae hard,
You hae tae ca' in sick.
Haud Hogmanay,
From yer kilt sportin' mukkers.

What Next?

2022 marked 10 years of Christmas Countdowns and 11 years since the first countdown. Having only missed 2017 it is quite an achievement looking back. In that time the countdowns have gone from a two week day-to-day poem to what it is now; 3 distinct countdowns for Christmas, New Year and Advent.

What comes next? The honest answer... I do not know. This was written in August 2023 and so far this year Pesky Publishing Ltd has been opened to formalise and professionalise what I've been doing for so long. The 2023 Christmas Countdown has already been started with several poems already written. What is weird is that by the time this book is in your hands, the 2023 countdown will have either started, be a thing of the past or worst, never made it to publishing.

At this moment the plan is to continue the Christmas Countdown for as long as I can naturally do it. The biggest limit at the moment is writing at least 31 unique poems about Christmas and New Year each year. To do this I listen to Christmas music in the summer and spread out the load over the last half of the year while avoiding reading old poems to prevent contamination.

Ultimately the decision to write comes from the existence of readers. Pesky Poetry has a worldwide audience, something I still struggle to come to terms with. When it started and the numbers were in the 10's or 100's of readers it was exciting, now that the readers are in the thousands it amazes me and makes me feel so loved. The community that read me are amazing and without them this whole project would not exist, a fact I remind myself of before making any decisions with Pesky Poetry and now Pesky Publishing.

You can stay up to date with the current and future plans by searching Pesky Poetry on your favourite search engine or visiting peskypoetry.com.

About The Author

William Fraser is better known as the Pesky Poet. He started out on the journey of writing in 2012 as a way of proving that his recent dyslexia identification did not mean the death of a writing career.

In the beginning there was Creatively Become Indifferent. This was a place to share random writing works starting with a stream of poems around the London Olympics. The first being about Tom Daley. Although some short stories and essays were published, it was clear early on that poetry was the best received form of writing. In 2016 Creatively Become Indifferent was closed and Pesky Poetry was opened marking a pivot to specialising in poetry. Since then Pesky Poetry has covered topics of all forms ranging from Unrequited Love and the Loss of Family.

William finds inspiration to write in everywhere, from his day job to sleeping. In the last five years William lost his father, an avid supporter and reader of his works. Only a couple of years later his grandfather also passed, leaving a big hole in his life.

www.ingramcontent.com/pod-product-compliance
Lightning Source LLC
Chambersburg PA
CBHW071216080526
44587CB00013BA/1394